Words Their Way

Within Word Pattern Sorts for Spanish-Speaking English Learners

Lori Helman
University of Minnesota

Donald R. Bear
Iowa State University

Marcia Invernizzi
University of Virginia

Shane Templeton
University of Nevada, Reno

Francine Johnston
University of North Carolina, Greensboro

PEARSON

Boston • Columbus • Indianapolis • New York • San Francisco • Upper Saddle River
Cape Town • Dubai • London • Madrid • Milan • Munich • Paris • Montreal • Toronto • Amsterdam
Sao Paulo • Sydney • Hong Kong • Seoul • Singapore • Taipei • Delhi • Tokyo • Mexico City

Vice President and Editor-in-Chief: Aurora Martínez Ramos
Associate Sponsoring Editor: Barbara Strickland
Editorial Assistant: Katherine Wiley
Senior Marketing Manager: Christine Gatchell
Production Editor: Janet Domingo
Projection Coordination, Editorial Services, and Text Design: Electronic Publishing Services, Inc., NYC
Manufacturing Buyer: Linda Sager
Art Rendering and Electronic Page Makeup: Jouve
Interior Design: Electronic Publishing Services, Inc., NYC

Credits and acknowledgments borrowed from other sources and reproduced, with permission, in this textbook appear on the appropriate page within text.

PEARSON

ISBN 10: 0-13-702872-5
ISBN 13: 978-0-13-702872-6

CONTENTS

UNIT 13

PREFACE

Words Their Way: Within Word Pattern Sorts for Spanish-Speaking English Learners is designed to supplement the text *Words Their Way with English Learners: Word Study for Phonics, Vocabulary, and Spelling*. That text provides a practical, research-based, and classroom-proven way to study words with students. This supplemental text provides a complete curriculum for within word pattern spellers from Spanish-speaking backgrounds by focusing on vocabulary development and linguistic commonalities and contrasts to support students as they learn English.

The curriculum outlined in this text is designed to scaffold students by (1) carefully pacing and sequencing word study learning from simple to more complex features; (2) starting with the most common and high-utility English words; (3) teaching vocabulary through pictures and word-picture matching; and (4) providing opportunities to build on the Spanish language skills that students bring from their home language.

Words Their Way: Within Word Pattern Sorts for Spanish-Speaking English Learners provides teachers with prepared reproducible sorts and step-by-step directions on how to guide students through the sorting lesson. There are literature connections, organizational tips, and follow-up activities to extend the lesson through weekly routines. The materials provided in this text will complement the use of an existing phonics, spelling, and reading curricula.

OVERVIEW

The ideas found in this text are based on the solid research and instructional practices outlined in *Words Their Way: Word Study for Phonics, Vocabulary, and Spelling.* In particular, *Words Their Way: Within Word Pattern Sorts for Spanish-Speaking English Learners* is a companion volume to the text *Words Their Way with English Learners: Word Study for Phonics, Vocabulary, and Spelling (WTW EL)*. It is a good idea to have this primary text on hand for its presentation of the research base; overview of developmental word knowledge; and assessments, additional sorts, and access to web-based support materials. Refer specifically to Chapter 6 in *WTW EL* for its collection of activities and picture and word sorts for students in the within word pattern stage of spelling.

SCOPE AND SEQUENCE OF THIS BOOK

This book begins with three concept sorts (Unit 1) that help students learn sorting procedures, teach important content words from typical primary-grade thematic units, and serve as pre-assessments of students' oral English skills. Unit 2 helps you review and assess students' ability to distinguish the long and short sounds of each vowel using pictures. In Unit 3, words and pictures are combined as students compare the spellings and sounds of CVC and CVCe words (e.g., *cap* and *cape*). In Unit 4 students immerse themselves in the study of the most common long-vowel patterns: CVCe and CVVC. Unit 5 focuses on additional patterns such as those in the words *stay, grow, sight,* and *gold*. Students have many opportunities to practice these numerous long-vowel patterns and should have a good grasp of them before moving on to other vowel sounds. Unit 6 introduces the concept of homophones while at the same time helping students review many words that are spelled with the CVCe and CVVC patterns.

In Unit 7, students are guided through *r*-influenced vowel sounds and their spellings. Continuing on into more difficult vowel patterns, Unit 8 addresses diphthongs such as in the words *coin* or *mouth* as well as words with vowel sounds that are neither short, long, nor *r*-influenced such as those in the words *tooth, hook, claw,* or *salt.* This portion of word study in the within word pattern stage becomes very cluttered with vowel patterns; thus it is important to provide clear and explicit instruction and ensure that students are able to make generalizations about the vowel patterns they are investigating.

Beginning in Unit 9 students move beyond the spelling of vowel patterns in words to other features of word study. Unit 9 concentrates on the sounds and spellings of complex consonant clusters such as in the words *wrist, street, shrub, bridge,* and *lunch.* Spanish speakers will not have experienced many of these sound-letter combinations in their home language, so extra focus and practice may be in order to identify their sounds and spelling patterns. In Unit 10, contractions are introduced, defined, and sorted according to their component parts. In this unit, grammar is highly connected to the study of individual words. Unit 11 revisits the concept of homophones, this time using multiple vowel patterns, such as in the words *ate/eight* and *grown/groan,* and students have many opportunities to review and practice the numerous vowel patterns they have studied throughout the within word pattern stage. This book concludes with two units (12 and 13) that bridge toward the syllables and affixes stage: an introduction to two-syllable high-frequency words and an introduction to inflectional endings for plural and past tense such as in the words *foxes* or *wanted.* When students have a good understanding of these features, they will be ready to move on to the study of multi-syllable words and the spelling processes that take place when meaningful word parts are joined.

RESOURCES

Each unit's Notes for the Teacher section provides placement guidelines and background information about the features of study. Introductory materials also describe standard weekly routines that ensure practice and enrichment, offer suggestions for games, and list relevant books in the Literature Connections features. Directions for how to introduce the sort, along with additional teaching tips, are provided for each lesson. Sorts are presented as black line masters that can be reproduced so that students can sort their words a number of times. We recommend that you enlarge the sorts about 10 percent to maximize the print size. You should also use the masters to prepare a set of pictures and words for modeling. These words could be shared with students using a document projector or other technology that you have available, or they can be enlarged for use in a pocket chart stand. See *WTW EL* for additional background information, organizational tips, games, and activities. The website has many electronic support materials such as videos, sorts, and games.

PLACEMENT AND PACING

This book contains 13 units of study that progress in difficulty from early to middle to late features in the within word pattern stage of spelling development. The first three sorts may be used with the whole class regardless of their spelling level—they are concept sorts that will teach sorting procedures and develop conceptual understanding of a variety of topics. Following are general guidelines for placing students, using the inventory results.

Early within word pattern spellers will know most short vowels and will be using but confusing silent vowel markers (e.g., writing WATE for *wait* or FLOTE for *float*). They may earn 0–2 points under "long vowels" on the Primary or Elementary Spelling Inventory. They will be ready to first contrast short- and long-vowel pictures in Sorts 4 to 8, and this work with sounds will help students with Sorts 10 to 14, which contrast CVC and CVCe words such as *hat* and *hate.*

Middle within word pattern spellers will receive a majority of points under the "long vowels" features on the spelling inventory, and may even earn points under "other vowels." They will benefit from the review of common long-vowel patterns and from an introduction to less common vowels in Sorts 21 to 40.

Late within word pattern spellers will spell most long vowels correctly (missing no more than one on the inventory) but will still make errors in the "other vowels" category. They might take a step back to review *r*-influenced vowels (Sorts 29 to 35) before moving to Sorts 36 to 40.

Each unit contains spell checks that can be used as pre-tests to gather more in-depth information about features and to place your students more accurately. For example, you might give Spell Check: Assessment for Short- and Long-Vowel (CVCe) Patterns (page 41) to students who are in the early within word pattern stage to determine whether they can spell words with the common CVCe pattern. If students get a score of 90 percent or better on the spell check, you can safely move on to the next feature or unit. If students spell between 50 and 75 percent of the words correctly on the pre-test, the words and features are at their instructional level. The spell checks are also designed to be post-tests to determine whether students have mastered and retained the features in each unit.

The sorts are designed at a relatively slow pace to ensure that students are not bombarded by too many new patterns at once, but it may not be necessary to do every sort if students demonstrate knowledge. The words have been selected to represent the highest frequency examples, as well as those words most commonly used in elementary content study. If you find that your students know the meanings of all of these words, feel free to substitute other words to extend their range of vocabulary. After introducing a sort, you should spend about a week following routines that encourage students to practice for mastery. An independent word study take-home task is included in the appendix to help students get additional work with the words. Through informal assessments of your students' sorting and writing you will see whether the pace you are following needs to be increased or slowed down. If additional sorts are needed to practice the feature under study, use the blank template in the appendix to create similar sorts using different words with the same feature. Additional words are included for most sorts to provide practice or challenge to students with a more developed reading vocabulary.

A FOCUS ON SPANISH-SPEAKING ENGLISH LEARNERS

This book has been written to focus specifically on the background knowledge and possible cross-linguistic confusions experienced by Spanish-speaking students. Notes throughout the text will help you be aware of the most challenging sound and spelling patterns for your students who speak Spanish, including those aspects of English that are not present in Spanish. When your students have difficulties with pronouncing the sounds of vowels or consonant clusters, we encourage you not to overemphasize these discrepancies—this will only discourage your students from speaking up. Instead, provide modeling, explicit instruction, and let your students compare what they notice about the sounds of English and Spanish.

English learners from non-Spanish-speaking backgrounds will likely also find the pace, scope, and sequence of this book helpful because it provides a focus on important, high-utility vocabulary; frequently uses pictures to teach new words; provides multiple opportunities to practice skills in a systematic manner; and gives the teacher control of how and when oddball words are introduced. For a longer discussion of these techniques and other ideas for supporting English learners in their classroom word study activities, see *WTW EL*.

ACKNOWLEDGMENTS

The author wishes to thank the following reviewer: Karen Banks, George Mason University.

unit 1

Concept Sorts for Vocabulary Development

Notes for the Teacher

A *concept sort* is an activity in which pictures, objects, or words are grouped by shared attributes. The three picture sorts in this unit are designed to build vocabulary, develop critical-thinking skills, and teach the process of sorting. Use one or more of these example sorts early in the school year to demonstrate and practice sorting routines. These sorts are especially useful in the content areas you are teaching; you can use them to informally assess your students' academic language skills in English. Consider creating a sort similar to the oceanic habitat example in this unit that fits with your classroom units of study. Watch to see whether students understand your directions for doing a sort and then categorize the pictures appropriately. Note how students sort the items when they have an opportunity to do a sort of their own categorizing. Are students able to describe their thinking in English? Do they use single words, phrases, or complete sentences? Which words do students know, and which will they need instruction to learn? Do they use home language resources to better understand the concepts and language involved with the sorts? Use these sorts to support your instruction in science, math, or social studies, and create other sorts based on the thematic studies in your classroom.

Standard Weekly Routines for Use With Sorts 1–3

1. **Learning and Practicing Unknown Vocabulary** First, discuss how the pictures connect to the content area studies in your classroom. Preview the pictures from the sort with your students. Name each picture, and have students repeat the name. Next, ask students to name the pictures. Set aside words that are unknown to be reviewed. Select up to ten of the unknown pictures for vocabulary study. Talk about the pictures with students, clarify their meanings with a student-friendly definition, and invite students to use the words in sentences. If possible, have students share the names of the pictures in Spanish.
2. **Repeated Work with the Pictures** Students should repeat the sort several times after it has been modeled and discussed under your direction. Make a copy of the blackline master for each student, enlarging it to make it more readable and reduce paper waste. Provide opportunities for students to create their own categories for the sort and to share

their ideas with others. After cutting out the pictures and using them for individual practice, store the pieces in an envelope or baggie to sort again several times on other days. See *WTW EL* for tips on managing picture sorting.

3. **Picture Hunts and Picture Dictionaries** Students can look through magazines, catalogs, and newspaper ads for pictures of things to add to their concept sorts. Encourage students to share their findings and create personal picture dictionaries so they can reference the vocabulary in the future.

4. **Games and Writing Activities** Many games, such as Concentration, I Spy, Charades, and Bingo, are outlined in *WTW EL* and will help you use the concept sort cards for vocabulary and language-development activities. Students can also pair up to quiz each other on the names of the pictures. Use the concept sorts as springboards for student writing projects.

Sort 1: Plant Parts

Items in the Plant Parts Concept Sort

root	**stem**	**leaf**
fruit	**flower**	(flower)
(cauliflower)	(stem)	(roots)
(corn)	(peach)	(carrots)
(celery)	(vine)	(grapes)
(rose)	(leaves)	(spinach)

Demonstrate, Sort, Check, and Reflect

1. Prepare a set of pictures from the Sort 1 images on page 8 for teacher-directed modeling. Practice the vocabulary with students as described earlier in the Standard Weekly Routines section.

2. Begin a concept sort by stating your thinking out loud as you model for your students. *"There are lots of pictures here of plant parts—roots, stems, leaves, fruits, and flowers. The words in dark letters are the labels for these groups. Let's make five groups with a word at the top of each column and then decide whether the plant part is a root, stem, leaf, fruit, or flower."* Hold up the picture of a flower. *"This is a picture of a _____? Flower, yes. A flower goes in the flower group. What about a peach? What part of a plant is a peach? The fruit, right!"* Now hold up something that is a little more challenging, such as the celery. *"This is a picture of celery. What part of a plant is the celery we eat? Have you ever seen little roots growing underneath this part of the celery? Or the leaves growing at the other end? This celery is the stem of a plant."* Continue working your way through each item to decide where it will go—in the root, stem, leaf, fruit, or flower group. Encourage students to participate in your decision making as you go. The completed sort should be categorized as follows:

   Root: roots, carrots
   Stem: stem, celery
   Leaf: vine, leaves, spinach
   Fruit: corn, peach, grapes
   Flower: flower, cauliflower, rose

FIGURE 1.1 Beginning of Plant Parts Concept Sort

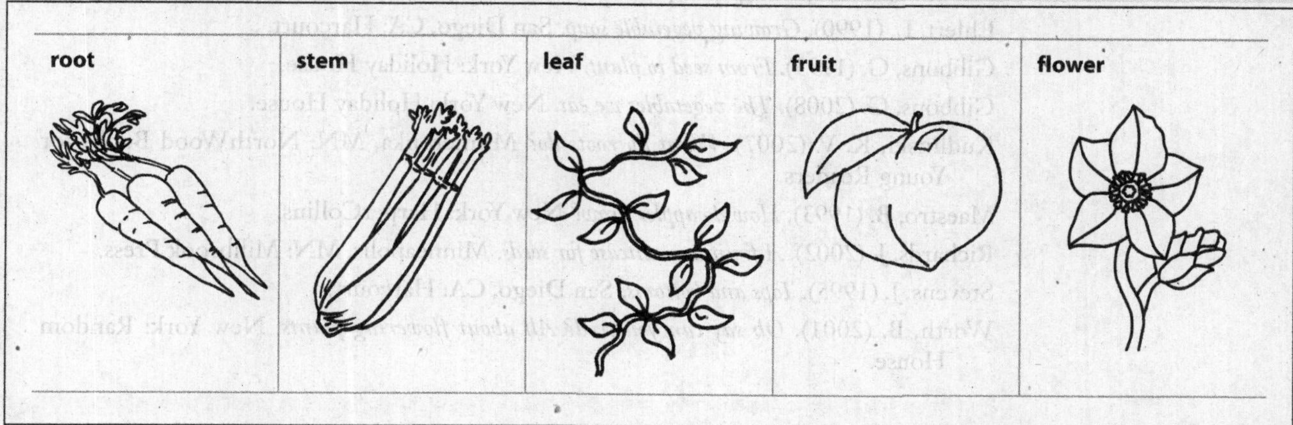

3. Next demonstrate how to check, correct, and reflect. *"When we are all done, we read our columns and check our work. If we find something that does not belong, we make a change."* Read the pictures in each column, adjusting if necessary. Restate why you sorted the way you did. The beginning of the plant parts concept sort is pictured in Figure 1.1.
4. Give students their own sets of plant part picture cards for use in sorting. Allow them to repeat the sort and then discuss their thinking with their classmates and you. Have them name the items in their groups and check them. Listen to the language your students use, and take advantage of opportunities to repeat the names of unknown words.

Extend

On subsequent days, ask students to find other pictures of plant parts. They can draw them or cut them out of magazines. Students can also write the names of specific plant parts and include more words in their sorts. Have them play guessing games in pairs to identify the names of the pictures. Put the picture and word cards in plastic bags for students to take home to practice with their families. If plant parts are included in your science curriculum, connect this sort to other class lessons. Have students glue the pictures into individual dictionaries or science notebooks to refer to as they learn new words in English. Read and discuss some of the pictures and stories from the following Literature Connection feature.

Literature Connection

Blevins, W. (2004). *Parts of a plant.* Mankato, MN: Compass Point Books.

Bodach, V. K. (2007). *Flowers (Plant Parts Series).* Mankato, MN: Capstone Press.

Bodach, V. K. (2007). *Fruits (Plant Parts Series).* Mankato, MN: Capstone Press.

Bodach, V. K. (2007). *Leaves (Plant Parts Series).* Mankato, MN: Capstone Press.

Bodach, V. K. (2008). *Roots (Plant Parts Series).* Mankato, MN: Capstone Press.

Bodach, V. K. (2008). *Stems (Plant Parts Series).* Mankato, MN: Capstone Press.

Bulla, C. R. (2001). *A tree is a plant.* New York: HarperCollins.

Cherry, L. (2003). *How groundhog's garden grew.* New York: Scholastic.

Cole, H. (1997). *Jack's garden.* New York: Mulberry Books.

Ehlert, L. (1990). *Growing vegetable soup.* San Diego, CA: Harcourt.

Gibbons, G. (1993). *From seed to plant.* New York: Holiday House.

Gibbons, G. (2008). *The vegetables we eat.* New York: Holiday House.

Kudlinski, K. V. (2007). *What do roots do?* Minnetonka, MN: NorthWood Books for Young Readers.

Maestro, B. (1993). *How do apples grow?* New York: HarperCollins.

Richards, J. (2002). *A fruit is a suitcase for seeds.* Minneapolis, MN: Millbrook Press.

Stevens, J. (1995). *Tops and bottoms.* San Diego, CA: Harcourt.

Worth, B. (2001). *Oh say can you seed? All about flowering plants.* New York: Random House.

Sort 2: Geometric Figures

Items in the Geometric Figures Sort

curved	**straight**	(circle)
(square)	(oval)	(figure eight)
(parallelogram)	(rectangle)	(quatrefoil)
(crescent)	(ellipse)	(trapezoid)
(rhombus)	(triangle)	(star shape)
(pentagon)	(octagon)	(hexagon)

Demonstrate, Sort, Check, and Reflect

1. Prepare a set of pictures from the Sort 2 images on page 9 for teacher-directed modeling. Practice the vocabulary with students as described earlier in the Standard Weekly Routines section.

2. Begin the concept sort by stating your thinking out loud as you model for your students. *"This sort has lots of pictures of shapes or geometric figures. Let's try sorting the figures by whether they have straight or curved sides. The words in dark letters are the labels for these groups:* curved *and* straight." Hold up the picture of a circle. *"This is a picture of a _____? Circle, yes. A circle has a curved side. I am going to put the circle under the word* curved *and we can put other pictures of curved shapes underneath. What about a rectangle? Does a rectangle have curved sides or straight sides? Straight sides, right."* Now pick up another geometric figure card, such as a parallelogram. *"This is a picture of a parallelogram. Does a parallelogram have curved or straight sides? Straight. Let's put the parallelogram below the rectangle because it also has straight sides."* Continue working your way through the figures to decide where each will go—underneath the word *curved* or *straight.* Encourage students to participate in your decision

making as you go. Remember to repeat the figure names that are more difficult many times as you sort them. The completed sort should be categorized as follows:

Curved: circle, oval, figure eight, quatrefoil, crescent, ellipse

Straight: square, parallelogram, rectangle, trapezoid, rhombus, triangle, star shape, pentagon, octagon, hexagon

3. Next demonstrate how to check, correct, and reflect. *"When we are all done, we read our columns and check our work. If we find something that does not belong, we make a change."* Read the pictures in each column, adjusting if necessary. Restate why you sorted the way you did.
4. Give students their own sets of geometric figure cards for use in sorting. Allow them to repeat the sort and then discuss their thinking with their classmates and you. Have them read the items in their groups and check them. Listen to the language your students use, and take advantage of opportunities to repeat the names of unknown words or build sentences with the words as students' language skills allow.

Extend

On subsequent days, ask students to think of other ways to sort their picture cards. Have them play guessing games in pairs to identify the names of the pictures. Share cognates in Spanish, such as *rectangle/rectángulo, hexagon/hexágono, rhombus/rombo,* or *parallelogram/paralelograma.* Put the picture cards in plastic bags for students to take home to practice with their families. Make a duplicate set of geometric figure cards to use in playing matching games. Look for objects in the environment and in print materials that have the same shapes as the geometric figures. Have the students create art projects using a variety of curved or straight-sided figures and then write stories about them. Read and discuss some of the pictures and stories from the following Literature Connection feature.

Literature Connection

Aboff, E. M. (2010). *If you were a polygon.* Mankato, MN: Capstone Press.

Aboff, E. M. (2010). *If you were a triangle.* Mankato, MN: Capstone Press.

Blaisdell, M. C. B. (2010). *If you were a circle.* Mankato, MN: Capstone Press.

Blaisdell, M. C. B. (2010). *If you were a quadrilateral.* Mankato, MN: Capstone Press.

Greene, R. G. (2001). *When a line bends . . . a shape begins.* Boston: Sandpiper Books.

Hoban, T. (1996). *Shapes, shapes, shapes.* New York: Greenwillow Books.

Johnson, S. T. (1995). *Alphabet city.* New York: Penguin Putnam, Inc.

Lionni, L. (1995). *Little Blue and Little Yellow.* New York: HarperCollins.

Metropolitan Museum of Art. (2005). *Museum shapes.* New York: Little, Brown Books for Young Readers.

Micklethwait, L. (2004). *I spy shapes in art.* New York: Greenwillow Books.

Pelletier, D. (1996). *The graphic alphabet.* New York: Scholastic.

Pluckrose, H. A. (1995). *Shape.* Danbury, CT: Children's Press.

Seuss, D. (1973). *The shape of me and other stuff.* New York: Random House Books for Young Readers.

Walsh, E. L. (2007). *Mouse shapes.* San Diego, CA: Harcourt.

Sort 3: Oceanic Habitat

Items in the Oceanic Habitat Sort

plant	animal	nonliving
(crab)	(kelp)	(rockweed)
(rock)	(shark)	(beach)
(zooplankton)	(sea otter)	(large fish)
(sea grass)	(Irish moss)	(small fish)
(shrimp)	(orca)	(boat)

Demonstrate, Sort, Check, and Reflect

1. Prepare a set of pictures from the Sort 3 images on page 10 for teacher-directed modeling. Practice the vocabulary with students as described earlier in the Standard Weekly Routines section.
2. Begin the concept sort by stating your thinking out loud as you model for your students. *"This sort has lots of pictures from an oceanic habitat. Some of these items represent living things like plants and animals. Others are not alive. Let's sort by whether the item is a plant, an animal, or a nonliving thing."* Demonstrate the sort as has been described for Sorts 1 and 2 earlier. The completed sort should be categorized as follows:

   Plant: kelp, rockweed, sea grass, Irish moss

   Animal: crab, shark, zooplankton, sea otter, large fish, small fish, shrimp, orca

   Nonliving: rock, beach, boat
3. Next check, correct, and reflect with the students. *"Let's read our columns and check our work. If we find something that does not belong, we will make a change."* Read the pictures in each column, adjusting if necessary. Restate why you sorted the way you did.
4. Give students their own sets of ocean picture cards for use in sorting. Allow them to repeat the sort and then discuss their thinking with their classmates and you. Have them read the items in their groups and check them. Listen to the language your students use, and take advantage of opportunities to repeat the names of unknown words or build sentences to extend students' language skills. Use some of the disciplinary language of science, such as *"A shark is similar to or different from a crab in the following ways . . ."*

Extend

- On subsequent days, ask students to think of other ways to sort their picture cards. Have them play guessing games in pairs to identify the names of the pictures. Put the picture cards in plastic bags for students to take home to practice with their families. Have students glue the pictures onto blank paper to create an underwater scene and then label their creations or write some descriptive statements about them. Enlarge the pictures and put them in a pocket chart along with their names for students to make connections between the oral and written words. Read and discuss some of the pictures and stories from the following Literature Connection feature.

Literature Connection

Dell, P. J. (2006). *Ocean plants.* Mankato, MN: Capstone Press.

Ganeri, A. (2003). *I wonder why the sea is salty and other questions about the oceans.* New York: Kingfisher Books.

Kranking, K. W. (2003). *The ocean is . . .* New York: Henry Holt & Co.

Ling, M. (2001). *Eye wonder: Oceans.* New York: DK Children.

Lugtu, C. J. L. (2004). *Life in an ocean.* Mankato, MN: Capstone Press.

Macken, J. E. (2005). *Water habitats/Habitats acuáticos: Beaches/Playas.* Milwaukee, WI: Weekly Reader Early Learning Library.

Pallotta, J. (2005). *Ocean counting: Odd numbers.* Watertown, MA: Charlesbridge.

Pitkin, L. (2003). *Journey under the sea.* New York: Oxford University Press.

Ring, S. (2005). *El océano.* Mankato, MN: Capstone Press.

Salas, L. P. (2007). *Oceans: Underwater worlds.* Mankato, MN: Picture Window Books.

Tagliaferro, L. (2007). *How many fish in the sea?* Mankato, MN: Capstone Press.

Ward, J. (2000). *Somewhere in the ocean.* Lanham, MD: Rising Moon.

SORTS 1–3

SORT 1: Plant Parts

root	stem	leaf
fruit	flower	

SORT 2: Geometric Figures

curved	straight	

SORT 3: *Oceanic Habitat*

plant	animal	nonliving

Assessment of Concept Sorts

Use the concept sorts to informally assess your students in three areas: vocabulary knowledge, sorting procedures, and content area learning. Consider the following questions:

1. **Vocabulary Knowledge** How many of the pictures can students identify? Are they able to say the words in English, in their home language, both, or neither? Do they use the words in simple sentences or have extended conversations about the items? Notice the level of word and sentence knowledge students have so that you can build on their abilities in future word-study activities.
2. **Knowledge of Sorting Procedures** Are students able to do the concept sorts on their own? Are they able to repeat the sort independently? Do they follow the procedures of checking and reflecting on their sorts? What aspects of the sorting process are difficult for them and may require further instruction?
3. **Content Knowledge** Do students demonstrate the content knowledge represented by the concept sorts? For example, have students correctly sorted the plant parts, geometric figures, and components of the oceanic habitat? Can students apply these understandings to new examples outside of the sort? What do their reflections or writings demonstrate about their learning?

unit

2

Picture Sorts Contrasting Short- and Long-Vowel Sounds

Notes for the Teacher

The picture sorts in this unit are designed to focus students' attention on the short and long sounds of each of the vowels and provide you with the assurance that your students are able to discriminate between the short and long sound of each vowel in single-syllable words before presenting the spelling patterns in upcoming units. The vowels are presented in an order that should be easiest for students from Spanish-speaking backgrounds, with the most difficult sounds (short *i* and short *e*) saved for last. If students have difficulty discriminating the vowel sound, take the time to help them stretch out and phonemically segment each word. If necessary, use sound boxes (Elkonin boxes) to isolate the vowel sounds or provide small mirrors for students so they can observe the position of their mouths as they say the distinct vowel sounds.

For students who correctly represent most short-vowel sounds in single-syllable words, Sorts 4–9 will provide a quick review of short- and long-vowel sounds prior to their study of the most common long-vowel spelling patterns in upcoming units. If students struggle with these picture sorts because they have difficulty discriminating between the vowel sounds, spend more time on each vowel contrast, refer to the key words for each of the vowel sounds and do additional sound segmentation activities for the words. It may also be helpful to create word cards that match the short-vowel pictures.

Standard Weekly Routines for Use with Sorts 4–9

1. **Learning and Practicing Unknown Vocabulary** Preview the pictures from the sort with your students. Name each picture, and have students repeat it. Next, ask students to name the pictures. Set aside words that are unknown to be practiced. Select up to ten of the unknown pictures for vocabulary study. Talk about the pictures with students, clarify their meanings with a student-friendly definition, and invite students to use the words in simple sentences that connect to their lives. If possible, have students share the names of the pictures in Spanish.
2. **Repeated Work with the Pictures** Students should repeat the sort several times after it has been modeled and discussed under your direction. Make a copy of the blackline master for each student, enlarging it to make it more readable and reduce paper waste. After cutting out

the pictures and using them for individual practice, store the pieces in an envelope or baggie to sort again several times on other days. See *WTW EL* for tips on managing picture sorting.

3. **Draw and Label and Cut and Paste** For seatwork, students can draw and label pictures of things that contain the targeted vowel sound. Refer students to the key words for each of the vowel sounds to consistently reinforce the vowel sounds. Students can look for pictures in magazines and catalogs and paste those into categories by vowel sound. They can also categorize, paste, and label the pictures from the blackline sort. This can serve as an assessment tool, but *do not* expect accurate spelling of the long-vowel pattern at this time.
4. **Word or Picture Hunts and Word Banks** Students can look through their word banks, catalogs, and reading materials for words or pictures of things that have the targeted vowel sounds. Plan a time for students to share their findings. Have students record words on a group chart or create individual collages of cut-out pictures that represent the vowel sounds being studied.
5. **Games and Other Activities** Many games outlined in *WTW EL* will help you use the sort cards for vocabulary and language-development activities. Variations of the Follow the Path game work well with vowel sounds. You might want to create one with all five long-vowel sounds.

Literature Connection

As you read books with your students, take time to introduce new vocabulary and compare the sounds of words. Look for books that highlight the vowel sound you are teaching, such as the titles in the following list. While or after you share the stories with students, have them chant along on phrases that highlight specific vowel sounds, such as "ape in a cape," "sky high fly pie," or "doodle flute."

Eichenberg, F. (1988). *Ape in a cape: An alphabet of odd animals.* New York: Sandpiper.

Hoberman, M. A. (2002). *Bill Grogan's goat.* New York: Little, Brown Books for Young Readers.

Nakagawa, C. (2008). *Who made this cake?* Honesdale, PA: Front Street.

O'Neill, A. (2002). *The recess queen.* New York: Scholastic.

Pinkwater, D. (1991). *Doodle flute.* New York: MacMillan Publishing.

Rylant, C. (1994). *Mr. Putter & Tabby bake the cake.* New York: Sandpiper.

Shaw, N. (1995). *Sheep out to eat.* New York: Sandpiper.

Shaw, N. (2003). *Raccoon tune.* New York: Henry Holt & Co.

Sierra, J. (2010). *Thelonius Monster's sky high fly pie.* Decorah, IA: Dragonfly Books.

Trapani, I. (2002). *Row, row, row your boat.* Watertown, MA: Charlesbridge Publishing.

White, N. (1999). *The magic school bus gets a bright idea: A book about light.* New York: Scholastic.

Demonstrate, Sort, Check, and Reflect

(See page 19.)

1. Prepare a set of pictures from the images at the end of this unit to use for teacher-directed modeling. Use the picture cards as headers and display the pictures randomly with picture side up. Practice the vocabulary of the pictures as described earlier in the standard weekly routines section. Place the two header cards on the table and make sure that students know their names.

2. Begin a sound sort by placing one picture into each column, explaining explicitly what you are doing. *"Here is a picture of a map. When I say* map *slowly, mmm-aaaa-p, I hear ă in the middle just like* cat. *So I will put* map *under the picture of the cat. This is a picture of a game. G-aaaa-mm has the sound of ā in the middle. The a says its name as in cc-aaaa-kk* (cake), *so I will put* game *under the picture of the cake."* Model one or two additional pictures as needed until students understand the task. Then invite them to participate in your sorting. *"Now who can help me sort the rest of these pictures?"* Continue with the students' help to sort all of the pictures. Let mistakes go for now. If students say the name of the word in Spanish, congratulate them and repeat the English label. Discuss whether the word would go into the same column if you were doing it in Spanish. Your sort will look something like the one shown in Figure 2.1.

3. When all the pictures have been sorted, read each picture in the columns and check for any that need to be changed. *"Do all of these sound alike in the middle? Do we need to move any?"*

4. Repeat the sort with the group. Keep the picture cards as headers. This time, you may want to mix up the pictures, turn them face down in a deck, and let students take turns drawing a card and sorting it in the correct column. You can also simply pass out the pictures and have the students take turns sorting them. Guide students to stretch out

FIGURE 2.1 Picture Sort Contrasting Short and Long Sounds of *a*

each word if they need help identifying the vowel sound. After sorting, model how to check by naming the pictures in each column and talking about how the words in each column are alike.

5. Give each student a copy of the sort for individual practice. Assign them the task of cutting out the pictures and then sorting on their own in the same way they did in the group. Give each student a plastic bag or envelope to store the pieces. On subsequent days, students should repeat the sorting activity several times. Involve the students in the other weekly routines described in Chapter 6 of *WTW EL* for the early within word pattern stage.

6. Informally assess the students on the vowel sounds under study throughout the unit. These sound sorts may not take a full week of study, so you may get to two in a single week. Observe students' accuracy and fluency in sorting and their knowledge of the English vocabulary. At the end of the unit, call out some of the items you have been working with, and ask students to show a "thumbs up" if the vowel sound in the middle makes the long sound (says its name).

Extend

Continue to work with any students who have difficulty identifying the short and long sounds of a given vowel. Periodically check in with students; ask them to separate a word into its individual sounds and to tell you whether the vowel sound is short or long (says its name). Consider creating a chart for the classroom where students post pictures of single-syllable words they find that contain one of the five long-vowel sounds.

Completed sorts for this unit are outlined in the following tables. Words in parentheses represent pictures.

Sort 4: Picture Sort Contrasting Short and Long Sounds of *a*

ă (cat)	**ā (cake)**
(man)	(game)
(hat)	(rain)
(graph)	(cave)
(bath)	(whale)
(flag)	(train)
(map)	(snake)
(bat)	(cane)
	(snail)
	(plate)

Sort 5: Picture Sort Contrasting Short and Long Sounds of *o*

ŏ (clock)	ō (bone)
(box)	(hose)
(doll)	(soap)
(dog)	(toes)
(lock)	(road)
(frog)	(nose)
(fox)	(goat)
(knot)	(smoke)
	(ghost)
	(boat)

Sort 6: Picture Sort Contrasting Short and Long Sounds of *u*

ŭ (cup)	ū (fruit)
(sun)	(shoe)
(gum)	(spoon)
(nut)	(mule)
(bug)	(cube)
(thumb)	(juice)
(plug)	(moon)
(duck)	(zoo)
(drum)	(flute)

Sort 7: Picture Sort Contrasting Short and Long Sounds of *i*

ĭ (pig)	ī (five)
(fish)	(bike)
(sick)	(dive)
(chin)	(drive)
(six)	(dice)
(swim)	(hive)
(kick)	(fire)
(hill)	(bride)
	(fly)
	(prize)

Sort 8: Picture Sort Contrasting Short and Long Sounds of *e*

ĕ (bed)	ē (feet)
(pen)	(wheel)
(desk)	(three)
(leg)	(leaf)
(hen)	(bee)
(nest)	(sweep)
(net)	(tree)
(ten)	(sheep)
	(seal)
	(peas)

Sort 9: Review of Long Vowels

ā (cake)	ē (feet)	ī (five)	ō (bone)	ū (fruit)
(cane)	(wheel)	(nine)	(rose)	(glue)
(chain)	(leaf)	(dive)	(cone)	(tube)
(whale)			(comb)	(zoo)

Spell Check: Assessment of Long-Vowel Sounds

(See page 25.) The spell check at the end of the unit can be used as a pretest and/or posttest to determine whether students can isolate and identify the medial long vowels. Name each picture and ask students to circle the letter that represents the vowel sound in the middle of each word. Students who score 10 or better can move on to the next set of words. If one particular vowel causes students trouble, take extra time to work with it before moving ahead. The spell check words are:

1. rain **2.** rope **3.** paint
4. bee **5.** slide **6.** road
7. suit **8.** nail **9.** teeth
10. goat **11.** juice **12.** fly

SORTS 4–9

SORT 4: Picture Sort Contrasting Short and Long Sounds of *a*

ă	ā	

SORT 5: Picture Sort Contrasting Short and Long Sounds of *o*

ŏ	ō	

SORT 6: Picture Sort Contrasting Short and Long Sounds of *u*

ŭ	ū	
	JUICE	
	SPEARMINT	

SORT 7: Picture Sort Contrasting Short and Long Sounds of *i*

ĭ	ī	

SORT 8: Picture Sort Contrasting Short and Long Sounds of *e*

SORT 9: Review of Long Vowels

ā	ē	ī
ō	ū	

SPELL CHECK: Long-Vowel Sounds

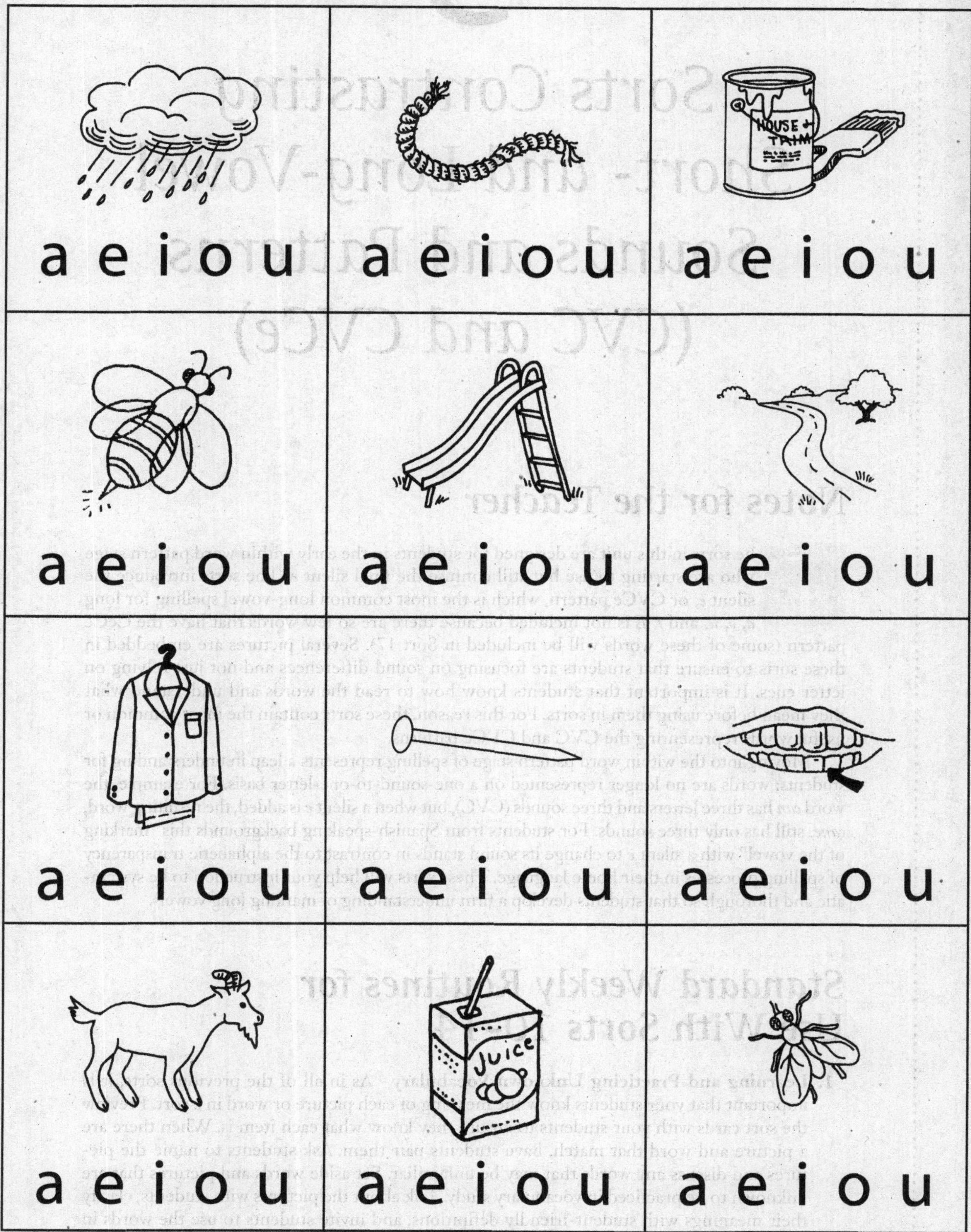

unit

3

Sorts Contrasting Short- and Long-Vowel Sounds and Patterns (CVC and CVCe)

Notes for the Teacher

The sorts in this unit are designed for students in the early within word pattern stage who are starting to use but still confuse the final silent *e*. The sorts introduce the silent *e*, or CVCe pattern, which is the most common long-vowel spelling for long *a*, *o*, *u*, and *i*. *E* is not included because there are so few words that have the CeCe pattern (some of these words will be included in Sort 17). Several pictures are embedded in these sorts to ensure that students are focusing on sound differences and not just relying on letter cues. It is important that students know how to read the words and understand what they mean before using them in sorts. For this reason, these sorts contain the most common or useful words representing the CVC and CVCe patterns.

Moving into the within word pattern stage of spelling represents a leap in understanding for students: words are no longer represented on a one-sound-to-one-letter basis. For example, the word *can* has three letters and three sounds (CVC), but when a silent *e* is added, the resulting word, *cane*, still has only three sounds. For students from Spanish-speaking backgrounds this "marking of the vowel" with a silent *e* to change its sound stands in contrast to the alphabetic transparency of spelling processes in their home language. These sorts will help your instruction to be systematic and thorough so that students develop a firm understanding of marking long vowels.

Standard Weekly Routines for Use With Sorts 10–14

1. **Learning and Practicing Unknown Vocabulary** As in all of the previous sorts, it is important that your students know the meaning of each picture or word in a sort. Preview the sort cards with your students to ensure they know what each item is. When there are a picture and word that match, have students pair them. Ask students to name the pictures and discuss any words that may be unfamiliar. Set aside words and pictures that are unknown to be practiced in vocabulary study. Talk about the pictures with students, clarify their meanings with student-friendly definitions, and invite students to use the words in

sentences that connect to their lives. If possible, have students share with each other in Spanish to clarify the meaning of any unknown items. Students could also draw simple pictures to remember the meanings of new words.

2. **Repeated Work with the Pictures and Words** Students should work with the featured sort several times after it has been modeled and discussed in a group. After cutting out the words and pictures and using them for individual practice, students can store the pieces in envelopes or baggies to sort again several times on other days. The pictures and words can also be used in partner activities during which students work together to read and spell the words. At some point, students may glue the sort onto paper or use it to combine with additional sorts in review lessons.

3. **Building, Blending, and Extending** Students should be able to read and spell these words, so they should practice doing both. Building, blending, and extending is an activity in which students spell with manipulatives. Use the building, blending, and extending cards with onsets and rimes on page 170 of this text for these activities. The cards can be enlarged for use in a pocket chart and can also be duplicated for use by individual students. Magnetic letters also work well, but the rime unit (e.g., *-ate*) should be kept together.

   For *building*, say the word and then model how to build it by putting together the onset and then the rime as shown in Figure 3.1. Compare the words with and without the silent *e*, such as *at* and *ate*. Let students compare the spelling patterns and how the words are pronounced. Then model how to change the onset to create other real or made-up words. For example, if *ch* is placed at the beginning of *at*, is it a word? Yes, *chat*. What about *ch* with *ate*? No, *chate* is not a word. Students can work with build, blend, and extend materials on their own or with a partner at their seats. They can keep track of real words they make in a word-study notebook.

   For *blending*, place the onset and rime in a pocket chart or write them on the board. Say the onset and then the rime as slowly as possible without distortion (e.g., /ch/ pause /aaaat/) pointing to the *ch* and then the *at* as a unit. Then say the word naturally as you run your hand under it or push the cards together: "*chat*." Model how you can change the rime to create a real or made-up word, such as *chate*. Have the students say the sounds with you and then individually. Do not isolate the vowel and the final sound. Students should learn these as units.

   For *extending*, include words in the blending activity from the list of additional words in each lesson. This will help students see that knowing a rime can help them figure out many additional words beyond the ones featured in the sort.

4. **Reading** Use decodable texts or short books that have a number of words with the featured family. Many publishers have created "phonics readers," and some of these focus on word families with CVCe or other long-vowel patterns. Be sure that students can read these books with at least 90 percent accuracy on a second reading and that they can understand the vocabulary. Screen the books for natural language patterns; stifled language such as, "It was the lone stone in the whole zone" will be difficult for English learners to make sense of because it does not sound like normal speech. Communicate the importance of text comprehension with students learning English, and ensure that they learn to ask questions when things fail to make sense.

5. **Word Recognition** After students have worked with the words and pictures for several days, hold up copies of the additional words and practice word recognition. Students can work in pairs to practice saying the words. Model blending of the onset and rime if students have trouble.

6. **Spelling** Hold up pictures one at a time and have the students spell the word using letter cards, chalkboards, white boards, or pencil and paper. Ask students to underline the letters

FIGURE 3.1 Building Short- and Long-Vowel Words

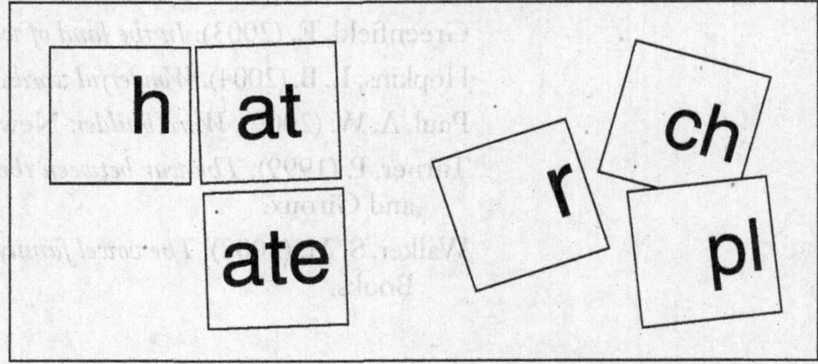

(such as *a* and *e*) that are the same in every word. Students can also work with a partner, taking turns calling a word for their partner to spell and then showing the word to check it.

7. **Word Hunts** Look for words in daily reading that mirror the featured vowel patterns. Challenge students to find others that could go in the group or brainstorm additional words, but understand that it may be difficult to find them on a word hunt. Create a list of rhyming words and have students discuss whether they are real words, made-up words, or if they don't know. When a word is unknown but fairly common and useful, consider spending instructional time to teach it. Such might be the case with a word like *fame.* When possible, spend your precious instructional time working on the essential words to support meaningful oral language and reading growth.

8. **Games and Other Activities** Create flip books, letter slides, or word wheels like those described in *WTW EL* for students to reread words in each rime family.

9. **Independent Word Study** Send home the directions for independent word study practice from the appendix of this text. Have students work with family members to do review and writing sorts and to reflect on their learning about words. Directions are included in both English and Spanish.

10. **Making the Sorts More Difficult with Oddballs** Words that do not follow the pattern under study have been intentionally left out of these sorts so that regularities are more apparent to students who are learning English. Once students grasp the vowel pattern under study, insert into the sort some of the "oddball" words located before the spell check as a way to check that students are not simply using visual cues to sort their words. You can control the level of difficulty of each sort by adding fewer or more oddballs.

11. **Assessment** To assess students' weekly mastery, ask them to spell and read the words. You can administer a traditional spelling test because the words in this unit feature a limited number of rime families, or you can dictate some of the featured words of the week for students to write down. Have students number their papers or white boards and call aloud a sample of words from the lesson. Spell checks are included at the end of this and future units and can serve as pre- or post-assessments.

Literature Connection

To help students develop a curiosity about how words change when letters are added or taken away, explore some of the following word play books. These books are doorways to discussing the expanding world of words that students are entering at this stage. Encourage students to be adventurous as they manipulate letters to create new words.

Banks, K. (2006). *Max's words.* New York: Farrar, Straus and Giroux.

Curtis, J. L. (2008). *Big words for little people.* New York: HarperCollins.

De Paola, T. (1999). *Andy: That's my name.* New York: Aladdin.

Falwell, C. (2006). *Word wizard.* New York: Sandpiper.

Greenfield, E. (2003). *In the land of words: New and selected poems.* New York: Amistad.

Hopkins, L. B. (2004). *Wonderful words.* New York: Simon & Schuster Children's Publishing.

Paul, A. W. (2009). *Word builder.* New York: Simon & Schuster Children's Publishing.

Turner, P. (1999). *The war between the vowels and the consonants.* New York: Farrar, Straus and Giroux.

Walker, S. M. (2008). *The vowel family: A tale of lost letters.* Minneapolis, MN: Carolrhoda Books.

Demonstrate, Sort, Check, and Reflect

(See pages 35–39.)

1. Prepare a set of pictures and words to use for teacher-directed modeling, such as for Sort 10: Word and Picture Sort Contrasting Short and Long Sounds of *a*.
2. Introduce the pictures and words and discuss any that are unfamiliar. Learn and practice unknown vocabulary words as described earlier in the standard weekly routines. Ask students if they notice anything about the words (i.e., they all have *a* in them). Ask about the vowel sounds in the middle of the words. Do they all have the same vowel sound? Model the segmentation process for several of the words or pictures if students do not easily distinguish the two vowel sounds. Introduce the short *a* symbol and the long *a* symbol that are part of the header cards. Place the picture of the *cat* and the *cake* as headers for the sort (see Sort 10 at the end of this unit). Explain that students need to listen for the vowel sounds in each picture or word and put each item under the correct header. Select a picture such as *map*. Ask, "*Does* map *have the same vowel sound as* cat *or* cake? *It has* ă *like* cat, *so we will put it under the cat.*" Do the same with a long-vowel word or picture, such as *gate*. "*Does* gate *have the same vowel sound as* cat *or* cake? *It has* ā *like* cake, *so we will put it under the cake.*" Continue with the students' help until all the pictures and words have been sorted. Let mistakes go for now.
3. When all the pictures and words have been sorted, have the students join in as you name them from top to bottom in the columns and check for any that need to be changed. "*Do all of these words sound alike in the middle? Do we need to move any?*" Ask the students how the words in each column are alike (one group has the sound of *ă* and the other group has the sound of *ā*).
4. Repeat the sort with the group. This time, you may want to mix up the words and pictures, turn them face down in a deck, and let students take turns drawing a card and sorting it into the correct column. You can also simply pass out the cards and have the students take turns sorting them. After sorting, model how to check by naming the words in each column and talking about how they are alike. This is a good opportunity to informally assess how easily your students can distinguish the medial vowel sounds.
5. Give each student a copy of the sort for individual practice. Assign the task of cutting out the words and pictures and then sorting on their own in the same way they did in the group. On subsequent days students should repeat the sorting activity several times. Involve the students in the other standard weekly routines described in this text and in *WTW EL* for the within word pattern stage.
6. Informally assess students on the vowel sounds under study throughout the week. Observe students' accuracy and fluency in sorting and their knowledge of the English vocabulary. At the end of the week, call out some of the words you have been working with, and ask students to think about whether the word needs a silent *e* or not.

Extend

Use the build, blend, and extend cards on page 170 to have students compare possible words that reflect the CVC or CVCe spelling patterns. Have students create lists of words that differ by only the final *e*.

Completed sorts for this chapter should look something like the following tables. Words in parentheses represent pictures. Additional words for the word families are listed after each sort.

Sort 10: Word and Picture Sort Contrasting Short and Long Sounds of *a* (CVC and CVCe)

ă (cat) cat	ā (cake) cake
(hat)	came
that	gate
(map)	name
jam	page
clap	safe
glad	made
(hand)	take
flat	(cave)
black	face
than	make
	gave
	(tape)

***Additional words:** last, fast, ask, mad, snack, grass, same, take, shade, whale, trade, base*

Sort 11: Word and Picture Sort Contrasting Short and Long Sounds of *o* (CVC and CVCe)

ŏ (clock) clock	ō (bone) bone
not	home
(frog)	(hose)
job	smoke
(lock)	pole
shop	broke

ŏ (clock) clock	ō (bone) bone
blob	phone
got	nose
drop	wrote
toss	cone
hot	(globe)
	note
	(stove)

Additional words: *rock, spot, shot, box, fox, soft, slot, knot, rope, hole, joke, stone, role, chose*

Sort 12: Word and Picture Sort Contrasting Short and Long Sounds of *u* (CVC and CVCe)

ŭ (cup) cup	ū (cube) cube
but	mule
much	cute
must	(flute)
(truck)	June
shut	flute
such	(tube)
(drum)	rude
junk	(mule)
stuff	use
(jump)	
rush	
just	
(bus)	

Additional words: *run, stuck, duck, lump, plum, club, mug, rule, tune, cube, prune, dude*

Sort 13: Word and Picture Sort Contrasting Short and Long Sounds of *i* (CVC and CVCe)

ĭ (pig) pig	ī (five) five
will	white
(fish)	like
(swim)	(vine)
kick	while
spin	dive
(kick)	write
thing	(nine)
think	(dive)
quit	vine
fill	twice
bring	
trip	

Additional words: *kit, bit, fit, sit, skit, slid, did, hid, wig, twig, size, bite, life, kite, line, dime, ripe, smile*

Sort 14: Review of Short versus Long Spelling Patterns (CVC and CVCe)

(See page 39.) Sort 14 is a review of the CVC and CVCe spelling patterns across the vowels *a, i, o,* and *u.* The label *CVC* refers to the words that have a short vowel in the middle and a consonant, consonant blend, or consonant digraph to the left and right of the vowel (e.g., *hat, flat, chat,* or *flash*). The label *CVCe* refers to the pattern of consonants and vowels with a silent *e* at the end to create a long-vowel sound.

Demonstrate, Sort, Check, and Reflect

1. Prepare a set of pictures and words to use for teacher-directed modeling. Introduce the headers—**CVC short** and **CVCe long**. Tell your students that they will be comparing and contrasting the short- and long-vowel spellings of the vowels they have been studying in the previous four sorts. Explain that *CVC* refers to the consonant-vowel-consonant

spelling pattern of the short vowels. Write several words on the board and label them to illustrate, such as *fat* = CVC. Words that have more than one consonant at the beginning or end surrounding a short vowel, such as *flat* or *flash*, will also be considered CVC words because they still have only the single short-vowel sound, and the blends or digraphs are acting as one unit. *CVCe* refers to the consonant-vowel-consonant-*e* spelling pattern of long vowels. Demonstrate the sorting process by saying each word and comparing it to each header. Have your students join you as you model sorting by pattern.

2. When all the words have been sorted, have the students join in as you name them from top to bottom in the columns and check for any that need to be changed. *"Do all of these words have the same vowel pattern? Do we need to move any?"* Ask the students how the words in each column are alike (one group has the pattern CVC and the other group has the pattern CVCe).

3. Follow steps 3–5 on page 29 as you did with the other vowel pattern sorts in this unit.

CVC short	CVCe long
(clock)	(cake)
(cat)	(five)
(pig)	(bone)
(cup)	(cube)
dot	place
plug	tune
flag	vote
crack	rule
sock	joke
nut	state
kid	smile

Additional words: *will, dig, grin, trick, clip, brick, thick, date, cave, wide, price, stone, phone, mule, cute*

Oddball Cards for CVCe Long-Vowel Spelling Patterns

(See page 40.) The oddball cards are provided so that you can selectively add them to students' sorts to make them more challenging. Oddballs help students see that not all CVCe words represent the long-vowel pattern and help ensure that students are correctly pronouncing and differentiating their words as they sort.

love	one	live
give	some	lose
done	none	whose
have	dance	come
chance	since	prince
gone	once	glove
prove	shove	move

Spell Check: Assessment for Short- and Long-Vowel (CVCe) Patterns

(See page 41.) This assessment evaluates students' understanding of the consonant-vowel-consonant (CVC) pattern and the spelling of long vowels following the consonant-vowel-consonant-silent *e* pattern (CVCe). Name each picture; then ask your students to think about each word's vowel sound and write the spelling of the word on the lines provided. Pictures are provided to reinforce students' understanding of the word you are saying. Following are the 18 words assessed:

1. cake	**2.** vine	**3.** man
4. rock	**5.** frog	**6.** nose
7. jump	**8.** lip	**9.** rope
10. bike	**11.** tube	**12.** desk
13. whale	**14.** flute	**15.** king
16. hand	**17.** gate	**18.** stove

SORTS 10–14

SORT 10: Word and Picture Sort Contrasting Short and Long Sounds of *a* (CVC and CVCe)

ă cat	ā cake	name
that		page
came	made	
gate	black	clap
glad	take	
safe	jam	face
	gave	than
flat		make

SORT 11: *Word and Picture Sort Contrasting Short and Long Sounds of o (CVC and CVCe)*

ŏ  clock	ō 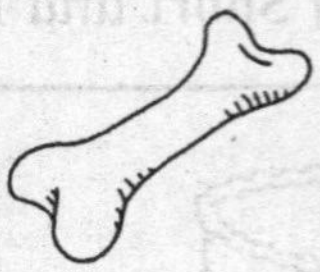 bone	blob
not		home
smoke	job	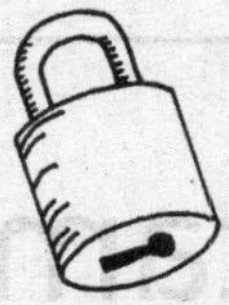
shop	broke	phone
pole	got	nose
	wrote	cone
note	toss	
hot		drop

SORT 12: Word and Picture Sort Contrasting Short and Long Sounds of *u* (CVC and CVCe)

ŭ  cup	ū  cube	but
mule	much	
must		rude
	June	rush
cute	flute	
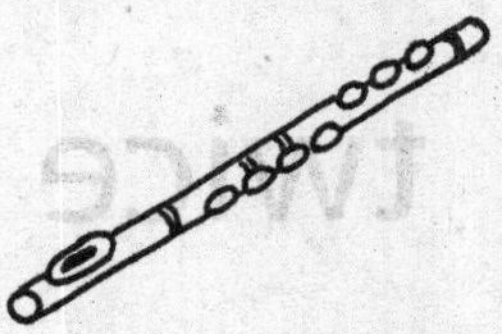	junk	just
shut	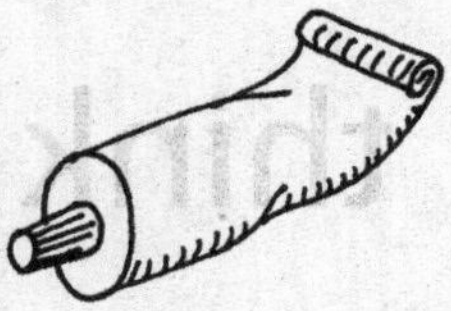	use
such	stuff	

SORT 13: *Word and Picture Sort Contrasting Short and Long Sounds of i* (CVC and CVCe)

ĭ pig	ī five	quit
kick	white	
like		fill
spin	dive	bring
	thing	vine
	write	twice
while	think	
will		trip

SORT 14: Review of Short versus Long Spelling Patterns (CVC and CVCe)

CVC short	**CVCe long**	
	vote	place
flag	plug	tune
rule	crack	dot
nut	joke	sock
kid	state	smile

Oddball Cards for CVCe Long-Vowel Spelling Patterns

love	one	live
give	some	lose
done	none	whose
have	dance	come
chance	since	prince
gone	once	glove
prove	shove	move

SPELL CHECK: **Assessment for Short- and Long-Vowel (CVCe) Patterns**

1. ______	**2.** ______
3. ______	**4.** ______
5. ______	**6.** ______
7. ______	**8.** ______
9. ______	**10.** ______
11. ______	**12.** ______
13. ______	**14.** ______
15. ______	**16.** ______
17. ______	**18.** ______

u n i t

4

Long-Vowel Spelling Patterns, Part 1 (CVCe and CVVC)

Notes for the Teacher

Sorts 15–19 are designed to help early-to-middle within word pattern spellers become familiar with and explicitly compare the CVCe and CVVC spelling patterns in common words. The CVVC pattern occurs with all of the vowels except *i*. We caution you to avoid teaching your students the old expression, "When two vowels go walking the first one does the talking." It works well with vowel digraphs like *ai*, *oa*, and *ea*, covered in these sorts, but it does not work with pairs like *ou*, *oo*, and *oy*, covered in later units. In this series of sorts, the CVVC pattern is compared to the CVCe pattern of the previous unit, and students come to see that there is more than one way to mark the long-vowel sound in a word.

Homophones—two words that sound the same but have different spellings—are common in these long-vowel words, so you will want to spend time with students talking about the meaning of the words they are working with and using them in sentences that clarify their meanings. Students may correctly pronounce a word but have an incorrect meaning in mind as they sort words that have homophone partners, such as *plain*, *meet*, or *tail*. In order for students to be successful in more advanced word study, it is important that they become familiar with the meanings of the correct spelling of a homophonic word. Because of the importance of learning and discriminating homophone partners, they are the word study focus in Unit 6 of this book, and in Unit 11 they are explored in even greater depth.

In their own writing, students may be confusing the spelling of long-vowel sounds in words, for example when they spell *snail* as SNALE or *stone* as STOAN. Students who are not yet marking the long vowel will not be ready for these sorts and will be more appropriately placed in Unit.3 of this book.

Finally, on occasion Spanish-speaking students learning to read and write in English may "sound out" the long *a* and long *o* in words as having two vowel sounds that slide together—a diphthong. If you see that students have represented the long *a* as EI or EY or the long *o* as OU in their writing, this is as likely to be a letter name-alphabetic error as a mistaken vowel pattern. When you see this, take the time to have students share their thinking out loud, and you will get a better sense of their developmental level.

Standard Weekly Routines for Use with Sorts 15–19

Pages 26–28 of this book outline a series of instructional practices to be used with the sorts including:

- learning and practicing unknown vocabulary
- working repeatedly with the sorts over the week
- building, blending, and extending sort words
- reading texts that feature the sort words
- providing word recognition practice with sort words
- spelling the words during informal assessments
- hunting for words with the featured pattern
- learning actively through games and hands-on projects

Please review pages 26–28 for an extended explanation of these activities. As in the previous unit, the current sorts may be made more difficult for students by including oddballs, or words that do not follow the long-vowel pattern under study. Once students grasp the CVVC and CVCe vowel patterns, insert some of the oddball words located on page 55 into the sort as a way to check that students are not simply using visual cues to sort the words. Instruct students to create an oddball category for words that do not have the long-vowel sounds. You can control the level of difficulty of each sort by adding fewer or more oddballs.

Finally, assessments should be done on a regular basis to gauge students' learning and to clarify their misconceptions. After each sort, ask students to spell selected words that follow the CVVC and CVCe patterns. You can do this in a traditional pencil-and-paper assessment or less formally on personal white boards during your small group lesson. A spell check is included in this unit to be used as a post-assessment before moving ahead into more complex vowel pattern study.

Literature Connection

To help students be metacognitive about the spelling patterns they see in simple long-vowel words, explore some of the following books or others on your bookshelves. Highlight some of the long-vowel pattern words that are used in the text, especially variations of the CVVC pattern, such as in the words *boat, green, train, sleep,* and *sea.*

Allen, P. (1996). *Who sank the boat?* New York: Putnam Juvenile.

Arnold, T. (1998). *Green Wilma.* New York: Puffin.

Brown, M. W. (2003). *Two little trains.* New York: HarperCollins.

Donaldson, J. (2003). *The snail and the whale.* New York: Puffin.

Jarman, J. (2008). *Class Three at sea.* Minneapolis, MN: Carolrhoda Books.

Marshall, E. (1994). *Three by the sea.* New York: Puffin.

Mortensen, L. (2009). *In the trees, honeybees.* Nevada City, CA: Dawn Publications.

Nelson, R. (2004). *Float and sink (First step nonfiction: forces and motion).* Minneapolis, MN: Lerner Classroom.

Prelutsky, J. (2008). *My parents think I'm sleeping (I can read book 3).* New York: HarperCollins.

Stewart, M. (2006). *Will it float or sink?* New York: Scholastic.

Demonstrate, Sort, Check, and Reflect

(See pages 50–54.) Prepare a set of words to use for teacher-directed modeling, such as for Sort 15: *Word Sort Contrasting Spelling Patterns for Long* a *(CVCe and CVVC)*.

1. Introduce the words in the sort and discuss any that are unfamiliar. Learn and practice unknown vocabulary words as described in the standard weekly routines on pages 26–28. Ask students what they notice about the sounds in the words (i.e., they all have the long *a* sound in the middle). Then ask them what they notice about how the words are spelled. If no one notices, point out that although the words all have the same sound in the middle, there are two spelling patterns that create the sound. Ask questions that guide students to see that some of the words are spelled using the silent *e* at the end, such as in the word *cake*. Others are spelled using a vowel "team," such as in the word *rain*. Introduce the header cards and show students that if they use the labels of *C* for consonant and *V* for vowel, these patterns may be represented as CVCe and CVVC. Hold up one word card at a time and have students help you sort it into the CVCe or CVVC column. *"Does* tail *have the CVVC pattern such as in* rain *or the CVCe pattern as in* cake*? Yes, it has the CVVC pattern, so we will put it under the word* rain." The beginning of your sort should look something like Figure 4.1. Continue with the students' help until all the words have been sorted. Let mistakes go for now.
2. When all the words have been sorted, have the students join in as you name them from top to bottom in the columns and check for any that need to be changed. *"Do all of these words have the CVCe pattern like* cake*? Do we need to move any?"* Ask how the words in each column are alike, helping students to articulate that the words have the same sound but different spelling patterns. Review what the CVCe and CVVC headers stand for and point out that when a blend or digraph starts or ends a word, it can be seen as a consonantal unit; thus, *brain* is still a CVVC word even though it technically has two consonants at the beginning.
3. Repeat the sort with the group. This time, you may want to mix up the words, turn them face down in a deck, and let students take turns drawing a card and sorting it in the correct column. You can also simply pass out the cards and have the students take turns sorting them. After sorting, model how to check by naming the words in each column and talking once again about how the words in each column are alike. This is a good opportunity to informally assess how easily your students can distinguish the CVCe and CVVC vowel patterns.

FIGURE 4.1 Sort 15 *Contrasting Spelling Patterns for Long* a

CVCe cake	CVVC rain
made	tail
place	wait
skate	main

4. Give each student a copy of the sort for individual practice. Assign the task of cutting out the words and pictures and then sorting on their own in the same way they did in the group. On subsequent days, students should repeat the sorting activity several times. Involve the students in the other standard weekly routines described in this text and in *WTW EL* for the within word pattern stage.
5. Informally assess students on the vowel patterns under study throughout the week. Observe students' accuracy and fluency in sorting and their knowledge of the English vocabulary. At the end of the week, call out some of the words you have been working with, and ask students to think about whether the word is an example of the CVVC or CVCe pattern.

Extend

Help imprint the appropriate spelling pattern of each long-vowel word by having students read the words numerous times over the course of the week. Opportunities for repeated readings come through games, word hunts, and reading and writing stories using the focus words. Once students grasp the vowel pattern under study, insert the oddball *said* into the sort as a way to check that students are not simply using visual cues to sort the words. Add only the number of oddballs that challenge but do not overwhelm your students.

Completed sorts for this unit should look something like the following tables.

Sort 15: Word Sort Contrasting Spelling Patterns for Long *a* (CVCe and CVVC)

CVCe cake (cake)	CVVC rain (rain)
shape	main
make	mail
taste	brain
skate	paid
place	snail
shade	tail
page	plain
age	wait
name	saint
made	
race	
take	
cave	

Additional words: *cape, gate, plane, same, safe, nail, gain, pail, fail, train*

Sort 16: Word Sort Contrasting Spelling Patterns for Long *o* (CVCe and CVVC)

CVCe bone (bone)	CVVC soap (soap)
home	loaf
those	goal
wrote	road
stone	groan
phone	float
zone	boat
code	coat
hope	toad
close	coach
vote	goat
drove	
whole	

Additional words: *note, joke, smoke, choke, hose, moan, soak, toast, loan, throat*

Sort 17: CVCe/CVVC Word Sort with Long *a, o,* and *e*

CVCe bone	CVVC soap
nose	wait
hope	main
Pete	toast
stole	waist
plate	speed
eve	boat
broke	deep
chase	paid

CVCe bone	CVVC soap
these	foam
	each
	seem
	train
	roam

Additional words: *tape, stone, wave, hole, sail, chain, coat, road, speak, treat*

Sort 18: Word Sort Contrasting Spelling Patterns for Long *u* (CVCe and CVVC)

CVCe cube	CVVC fruit	CVVC spoon
use	suit	room
tune	juice	cool
cute	bruise	food
rule	cruise	tooth
June		scoop
tube		gloom
huge		tool
flute		noon
rude		

Additional words: *mule, zoom, coop*

Sort 19: Review of CVCe and CVVC Long-Vowel Spelling Patterns

(See page 54.) This sort is a review of the CVVC and CVCe spelling patterns across the vowels *a*, *e*, *o*, and *u*. The label *CVVC* refers to the words that have two vowels making a long-vowel sound in the middle and a consonant, consonant blend, or consonant digraph to the left and right of the vowel pair (e.g., *teach, soap, fruit*). The label *CVCe* refers to the pattern of consonants and vowels with a silent *e* at the end to create a long-vowel sound.

Demonstrate, Sort, Check, and Reflect

1. Prepare a set of sort words to use for teacher-directed modeling. Introduce the headers—**CVCe cake** and **CVVC feet.** Tell your students that they will be comparing two of the ways that long-vowel spellings are made, applying what they have been learning over the past few sorts. Remind students that CVCe refers to the consonant-vowel-consonant-silent *e* spelling pattern that makes a long sound. Write several words on the board and label them to illustrate, such as *bone* = CVCe. Words that have more than one consonant at the beginning or end surrounding a short vowel, such as *write* or *phone,* will also be considered CVCe words because they still only have the single vowel and the final silent *e,* and the blends or digraphs are acting as one unit. The *CVVC* refers to the consonant-vowel-vowel-consonant spelling pattern of long vowels in words such as *feet.* Demonstrate the sorting process by saying each word and comparing it to each header. Have your students join you as you model sorting by pattern.
2. When all the words have been sorted, have the students join in as you name them from top to bottom in the columns and check for any that need to be changed. *"Do all of these words have the same vowel pattern? Do we need to move any?"* Ask the students how the words in each column are alike (one group has the pattern CVVC and the other group has the pattern CVCe).
3. Follow steps 3-5 on pages 44–45 as you did with the other vowel pattern sorts in this unit.

CVCe cake	CVVC feet
bone	fruit
size	soap
cube	spoon
wake	road
nice	paid
dude	trail
fake	broom
five	teach
phone	rain
write	meet
price	weed

Additional words: *page, race, eve, rice, rope, vote, mail, heat, boat, roam, suit*

Oddball Cards for Long-Vowel Spelling Patterns

(See page 55.) The oddball cards are provided so that you can selectively add them to make students' sorts more challenging. Oddballs help students see that not all CVVC and CVCe words represent the long-vowel pattern and help ensure that students are correctly pronouncing and differentiating their words as they sort.

love	one	live
give	some	lose
done	none	bread
dead	whose	come
you	once	been
great	build	their
they	said	friend
there	were	good

Spell Check: Assessment for CVCe and CVVC Long-Vowel Spelling Patterns

(See page 56.) This assessment is presented in a word-recognition format and checks for the correct spelling pattern of 18 CVCe and CVVC long-vowel words. Photocopy page 56 for all students you wish to participate in the assessment. Name each picture, then ask your students to circle the word next to each picture that matches the correct spelling pattern. Following are the 18 words assessed:

1. goat
2. cape
3. tube
4. braid
5. gate
6. dive
7. tooth
8. rain
9. rope
10. bike
11. leaf
12. cone
13. whale
14. flute
15. feet
16. fruit
17. pail
18. stove

SORTS 15–19

SORT 15: Word Sort Contrasting Spelling Patterns for Long *a* (CVCe and CVVC)

CVCe cake 	CVVC rain 	made
shape	tail	age
make	name	taste
wait	main	brain
skate	race	paid
place	saint	take
mail	cave	snail
page	plain	shade

SORT 16: Word Sort Contrasting Spelling Patterns for Long *o* (CVCe and CVVC)

CVCe bone	CVVC soap	home
boat	code	loaf
those	goal	hope
wrote	close	coat
road	stone	toad
vote	groan	phone
drove	float	coach
goat	zone	whole

SORT 17: CVCe/CVVC Word Sort with Long *a, o,* and *e*

CVCe bone	**CVVC soap**	wait
eve	nose	paid
toast	main	foam
hope	each	waist
seem	broke	Pete
chase	these	speed
train	stole	boat
roam	deep	plate

SORT 18: Word Sort Contrasting Spelling Patterns for Long *u* (CVCe and CVVC)

CVCe cube	CVVC fruit	CVVC spoon
use	suit	room
food	cool	bruise
June	cute	juice
tube	noon	gloom
rule	cruise	tool
tooth	huge	flute
tune	scoop	rude

SORT 19: Review of CVCe and CVVC Long-Vowel Spelling Patterns

CVCe cake	**CVVC feet**	five
bone	fruit	cube
spoon	soap	rain
road	phone	wake
trail	write	meet
nice	paid	fake
dude	size	weed
teach	broom	price

Oddball Cards for Long-Vowel Spelling Patterns

love	one	live
give	some	lose
done	none	bread
dead	whose	come
you	once	been
great	build	their
they	said	friend
there	were	good

SPELL CHECK: Assessment for CVCe and CVVC Long-Vowel Spelling Patterns

1. goat gout gote	**2.** caep caip cape
3. toob tube tub	**4.** bade braid brad
5. gait gatt gate	**6.** dive diiv diev
7. tuthe tothe tooth	**8.** rane rain reyn
9. rop roap rope	**10.** bike baik bick
11. leef leaf life	**12.** coon cohn cone
13. wheel whale whail	**14.** floot flut flute
15. fete feat feet	**16.** fruit froot frute
17. peil pail pale	**18.** stoov stouv stove

Long-Vowel Spelling Patterns, Part 2

Notes for the Teacher

The series of word sorts in this unit builds on students' knowledge of the CVCe and CVVC long-vowel patterns and extends this foundational knowledge to include less common long-vowel patterns such as those in the words *play*, *chew*, *high*, *kind*, or *fold*. These sorts are designed for students who are approaching the middle of the within word pattern stage and are typically having success with the CVCe pattern (e.g., *mice*, *huge*) and the CVVC pattern (e.g., *rain*, *toad*). Students at this stage may represent less common long-vowel patterns in a way they know how, such as spelling *fright* as FRITE or *chewed* as CHUDE. Students may also use but confuse long-vowel patterns in new ways, such as spelling *float* as FLOWT.

Teaching Spanish-speaking students systematically and explicitly throughout the within word pattern stage is essential to their continued writing success. If too many patterns are thrown at students without enough opportunities to practice, discuss, and internalize them, students may come to feel overwhelmed by the increasing complexity of the English spelling system. Pace your instruction so that students feel challenged but not inundated. Continually assess your students' understanding of the new vowel patterns being studied, and when necessary spend extra time reviewing sorts, going on word hunts, and extending word study with reading and writing projects before moving on. If you find that your students are not grasping the new material, or that they begin to confuse short- and long-vowel patterns in their writing, take a step back to review those more basic patterns before continuing in this unit.

Standard Weekly Routines for Use with Sorts 20–25

Follow the series of procedures outlined on pages 26–28 with these sorts, including learning and practicing the vocabulary, working repeatedly with the sorts, providing extension and at-home activities, and conducting informal assessments. A spell check is included in this unit as a post-assessment. However, given the number of patterns introduced here, it is important to be constantly assessing students' understanding of the new material. Regularly ask students to spell sample words as you work with them in small groups, and build in opportunities for them to

Literature Connection

Many good read-aloud books or beginning reading texts for students use words with a variety of long-vowel patterns. As you share these books with students, notice the many common words that use the patterns under study in this unit, such as *fly*, *night*, *play*, *flew*, *crow*, *kind*, and *gold*. Point out and discuss these words after you have shared a book together. Connect what students are reading to their word study, learning through books such as the following.

Baylor, B. (1986). *The way to start a day*. New York: Aladdin.

Eastman, P. D. (1958). *Sam and the firefly*. New York: Random House Books for Young Readers.

Gorbachev, V. (2009). *Molly who flew away*. New York: Philomel.

Hamilton, V. (2000). *The girl who spun gold*. New York: Blue Sky Press.

Murphy, M. (2004). *How kind!* London: Walker Books Ltd.

Ward, J. (2005). *Forest night, forest bright*. Nevada City, CA: Dawn Publications.

Yashima, T. (1976). *Crow boy*. New York: Puffin.

Yolen, J. (2000). *How does a dinosaur say good night?* New York: Blue Sky Press.

reflect on what they are learning either orally or in writing following a sorting session. Ongoing assessment is a great way for you to catch misconceptions and provide needed support.

Demonstrate, Sort, Check, and Reflect

(See pages 64–69.) Prepare a set of words to use for teacher-directed modeling, such as for Sort 20: *Word Sort Contrasting Spelling Patterns for Long* i *(CVCe and CV/CVV)*.

1. Introduce the words in the sort and discuss any that are unfamiliar. Learn and practice unknown vocabulary words as described in the standard weekly routines on pages 26–28. Ask students what they notice about the words (they all have the long *i* sound). Ask them what they notice about the spelling of the words and help them see that some of the words are spelled using the silent *e* at the end, such as in the word *five*. Others are spelled using a *y* or *ie*, such as in the words *by* or *tie*. Introduce the header cards and show students that if they use the labels of *C* for consonant and *V* for vowel, these patterns may be represented as CVCe and CV/CVV. When a blend or digraph starts or ends a word, it can be seen as a consonantal unit; thus, *sky* is still a CV word even though it technically has two consonants at the beginning. Hold up one word card at a time and have students help you sort it into the CVCe or CV/CVV column. "*Does my have the CVCe pattern such as in* five *or the CV/CVV pattern as in* by *or* tie? *Yes, it has the CV/CVV pattern, so we will put it under the word* by." Continue with the students' help until all the words have been sorted. Let mistakes go for now.
2. When all the words have been sorted, have the students join in as you name them from top to bottom in the columns and check for any that need to be changed. "*Do all of these words have the CVCe pattern like* five? *Do we need to move any?*" Discuss how the words all have the same vowel sound but that distinct patterns spell the sound.
3. Repeat the sort with the group. This time, you may want to mix up the words, turn them face down in a deck, and let students take turns drawing a card and sorting it into the correct column. You can also simply pass out the cards and have the students take turns sorting them. After sorting, model how to check by naming the words in each column and talking about how the words in each column are alike. This is a good opportunity to

informally assess whether your students are having difficulty distinguishing the CVCe and CV/CVV vowel patterns.

4. Give each student a copy of the sort for individual practice. Assign the task of cutting out the words and then sorting on their own in the same way they did in the group. On subsequent days, students should repeat the sorting activity several times. Involve the students in the other standard weekly routines described in this text and in *WTW EL* for the within word pattern stage.

5. Informally assess students on the vowel patterns under study throughout the week. Observe students' accuracy and fluency in sorting and their knowledge of the English vocabulary. At the end of the week, call out some of the words you have been working with, and ask students to think about whether the word is an example of the CVCe or CV/CVV pattern.

Extend

Provide numerous opportunities for students to read, write, and engage with the words in the sorts. Board games and card games are especially fun ways to review the words and talk about their spelling patterns.

Completed sorts for this chapter should look something like the following tables. Notes specific to individual sorts are included above each table of sorted words.

Sort 20: Word Sort Contrasting Spelling Patterns for Long *i* (CVCe and CV/CVV)

(See page 64.)

CVCe five	CV/CVV by, tie
nine	try
write	sky
hive	lie
line	shy
ripe	my
bite	fry
while	why
fine	fly
lime	dry
ice	die
mile	
hike	

Additional words: *like, bike, dime, time, drive, pie, cry, sly, spy, hi*

Sort 21: Word Sort with *a_e, ai,* and *ay*

(See page 65.) This sort adds another common spelling pattern to students' repertoires for long *a* words—*ay*. Follow the procedures listed in Demonstrate, Sort, Check, and Reflect and Extend outlined on pages 58–59, but set up three columns for the CVCe, CVVC, and CVV spelling patterns.

CVCe cake	CVVC rain	CVV day
shape	pain	play
ape	claim	say
name	waist	may
trace	brain	stay
bake	raid	way
stage		lay
tame		tray
plane		clay

***Additional words:** base, cave, taste, blame, wait, train, paint, gain, gray, slay, hay, spray*

Sort 22: Word Sort with *o_e, oa,* and *ow*

(See page 66.) This sort adds another common spelling pattern to students' repertoires for long *o* words—*ow*. Follow the procedures listed in Demonstrate, Sort, Check, and Reflect and Extend outlined on pages 58–59, but set up three columns for the CVCe, CVVC, and CVV spelling patterns.

CVCe bone	CVVC soap	CVV low
stole	loaf	grow
whole	roam	slow
code	road	show
dome	toad	know
broke	load	snow
robe	moan	throw
note		flow
hope		

***Additional words:** nose, hole, vote, globe, coat, float, throat, soak, crow, blow, throw, tow*

Sort 23: Word Sort with *u_e, ew,* and *ue*

(See page 67.) This sort adds more common spelling patterns to students' repertoires for long *u* words—*ew* and *ue*. Follow the procedures listed in Demonstrate, Sort, Check, and Reflect and Extend outlined on pages 58–59, but set up three columns for the CVCe *cube*, CVV *new*, and CVV *blue* spelling patterns.

CVCe cube	CVV new	CVV blue
tube	chew	glue
dude	grew	due
cute	knew	cue
tune	few	clue
mule	stew	sue
crude	blew	true
huge	threw	
	crew	

Additional words: *rude, flute, June, rule, drew, flew, screw, crew, flue, hue*

Sort 24: Word Sort Contrasting Spelling Patterns for Long *i* (*i_e, -igh,* and *-y*)

(See page 68.) This sort adds another common spelling pattern to students' repertoires for long *i* words—*igh*. Follow the procedures listed in Demonstrate, Sort, Check, and Reflect and Extend outlined on pages 58–59, but set up three columns for the CVCe, VCC, and CV spelling patterns.

CVCe five	VCC high	CV by
rice	sigh	my
ripe	thigh	why
kite	fight	cry
smile	might	dry
drive	night	fly
nine	sight	shy
mice	bright	
	right	

Additional words: *tribe, prize, stripe, pride, light, tight, flight, slight, try, sly, sky, spy*

Sort 25: Word Sort with Long *i* (CVCC) and Long *o* (CVCC)

(See page 69.) This sort focuses on two additional CVCC patterns: long *i* as in *child* and long *o* as in *cold*. Follow the procedures listed in Demonstrate, Sort, Check, and Reflect and Extend outlined on pages 58–59, but note for students that the similarity across the words is that they have a single vowel and two consonants at the end. The words each have a long-vowel sound, and you will sort them by whether they have the long *i* sound or the long *o* sound. After demonstrating, sorting, and checking, reflect with students on how they will remember that these words have the long sound even though they are similar to the CVC short-vowel spelling pattern as in *soft* and *list*. When students are comfortable with this sort, you might consider adding some short-vowel words and the headers **CVC short vowel *i*** and **CVC short vowel *o*** to challenge them.

CVCC child	CVCC cold
find	bold
blind	scold
wild	both
mind	most
mild	told
climb	gold
kind	jolt
	host
	post
	bolt
	ghost
	colt
	roll
	mold
	poll

Additional words: *grind, hind, sign, bind, hold, old, fold, folk, volt*

Spell Check: Assessment for CVCe, CV, and CVV Long-Vowel Spelling Patterns

(See page 70.) This spell check provides a quick assessment of the vowel patterns studied in this unit through a word-recognition format. Photocopy page 70 for all students you wish to participate in the assessment. Name each picture, then ask your students to circle the word under each picture that matches the correct spelling pattern. Following are the 12 words assessed:

1. kite
2. ghost
3. snow
4. mule
5. cave
6. home
7. bowl
8. glue
9. fly
10. lie
11. sky
12. threw

SORTS 20–25

SORT 20: Word Sort Contrasting Spelling Patterns for Long *i* (CVCe and CV/CVV)

CVCe five	CV/CVV by, tie	my
nine	try	why
fly	write	lime
hive	ripe	dry
line	shy	ice
sky	fine	mile
bite	fry	hike
lie	while	die

SORT 21: Word Sort with *a_e, ai,* and *ay*

CVCe cake	CVVC rain	CVV day
may	name	brain
ape	play	say
claim	trace	plane
lay	shape	raid
bake	stay	way
clay	stage	pain
tame	waist	tray

SORT 22: Word Sort with *o_e, oa,* and *ow*

CVCe bone	**CVVC soap**	**CVV low**
stole	grow	roam
slow	road	whole
toad	code	know
broke	show	loaf
snow	robe	dome
throw	load	note
hope	flow	moan

SORT 23: Word Sort with *u_e, ew,* and *ue*

CVCe cube	CVV new	CVV blue
chew	due	tube
tune	few	clue
glue	dude	knew
crude	grew	true
stew	cute	sue
huge	cue	threw
mule	blew	crew

SORT 24: Word Sort Contrasting Spelling Patterns for Long *i* (*i_e, -igh,* and *-y*)

CVCe five	VCC high	CV by
sigh	my	thigh
might	night	fly
nine	why	rice
dry	drive	fight
mice	kite	ripe
sight	bright	cry
shy	smile	right

SORT 25: Word Sort with Long *i* (CVCC) and Long *o* (CVCC)

CVCC child	**CVCC cold**	find
most	told	both
gold	wild	scold
post	jolt	bold
kind	host	blind
ghost	mind	colt
mold	bolt	roll
poll	mild	climb

SPELL CHECK: Assessment for CVCe, CV, and CVV Long-Vowel Spelling Patterns

kite kyt	ghost gowst	sno snow
muwl mule	cave cayv	howm home
bowl bole	glew glue	fly fliy
liy lie	sky skay	thrue threw

unit 6

Introduction to Homophones

Notes for the Teacher

Homophones are words that sound the same but have different meanings, such as the words *meat* and *meet.* Many of the words students have been sorting in the past few units of this text are homophones, and you have likely had conversations as you discussed the meanings of words together in class. Perhaps you have found yourself explaining to students, "No, not that kind of mail; this *male* means a boy," and so on. For students learning English as a new language, word sorting is always connected to vocabulary instruction, and homophones present a rich opportunity to learn new words. Homophones also add a layer of complexity to spelling—students must identify what a word means so that they can attach the correct spelling pattern to it. This unit directly addresses the concept of homophones and invites you to engage in many activities that will help students understand them better.

There are three sorts and a spell check in this unit. Two of the sorts examine common homophones that use the spelling patterns students have studied. The first of these sorts compares homophones that vary by the CVCe and CVVC spelling patterns, such as *tale* and *tail.* The second sort compares homophones that have *ee* or *ea* as the vowel pattern, such as *heel* and *heal.* As students work with these sets of simple homophones, they begin to develop an understanding of the connection between how a word is spoken, what the set of sounds may mean, and how the meaning influences a word's spelling. The third sort in this chapter is a homophone sort in Spanish and is provided as a resource for you to use with bi-literate students. The concept of what a homophone is may be made clearer to students if they learn that homophones exist in Spanish and have a chance to see examples in their home language.

This chapter is intended as an introduction to homophones and is designed to reinforce students' work with the common long-vowel patterns previously studied. After completing these sorts, your students should have a working knowledge of what a homophone is and why it is important to know *which* word you mean before it can be correctly spelled. A more in-depth exploration of homophones will come at the end of the within word pattern stage in Unit 11 of this text. At that point, the focus of word study will be to pull students toward a thoughtful understanding of how meaning influences the way words are composed in English.

Standard Weekly Routines for Use With Sorts 26–28

1. **Learning and Practicing Unknown Vocabulary** As in all of the previous sorts, it is important that your students know the meaning of each word in a sort. Preview the sort cards with your students to ensure they know what each item is. To clarify word meanings,

you might ask students to draw a picture on the back of the word card. For example, on the back of the *lone* card, a student might draw a person standing by herself. On the back of the *loan* card, a student might draw some dollar signs to remind herself that money is often loaned. Take the time to discuss all of the words and compare the meanings of the homophone pairs. It may be wise to start with half of the sorting words on the first day and add new pairs each day. This will allow you to practice the vocabulary within the word study lesson. Talk about the words with students, clarify their meanings, and invite students to use them in sentences that connect to their lives. If possible, have students share with each other in Spanish to clarify the meaning of any unknown items.

2. **Repeated Work with the Words** Students should work with the featured sort several times after it has been modeled and discussed in a group. After cutting out the words and using them for individual practice, students can store the pieces in envelopes or baggies to sort again several times on other days. The pictures and words can also be used in partner activities during which students work together to read and spell the words. At some point, students may glue the sort onto paper or use it to combine with additional sorts in review lessons.

3. **Writing** Invite students to create sentences that show they know the meanings of the homophone pairs and that they are using the appropriate spelling pattern, such as *I found a sail boat at the sale*. Consider creating group books or personal homophone dictionaries that teach the spellings and meanings of simple homophones. Be sure to check in with students each time they are comparing homophone pairs to make sure they understand what each word refers to.

4. **Spelling** As you work with the sort over the course of a week, have students quiz each other on the sounds, spellings, and meanings of the homophone pairs. Have them help each other think of ways to remember which word means what. Have students use their homophone dictionaries as a check.

5. **Games and Other Activities** Create matching games or silly stories, or build words with letter tiles to reinforce how the spelling of a homophone determines its meaning. Encourage students to notice homophones they encounter in their reading materials.

6. **Assessment** To assess students' weekly mastery, ask them to spell and read the words. Since there is a limited number of homophones, you can give a traditional spelling test using the words or you can dictate some of the featured words of the week. Have students number their papers or white boards, and call aloud a sample of words from the lesson. Discuss any words that are spelled with the incorrect homophone partner. A spell check is included at the end of this unit and is intended to serve as a post-assessment.

Literature Connection

The following books feature simple homophones in playful ways. Use these books or others that you know of as conversation starters to reinforce the concept of homophones. The pictures will help students learn new vocabulary and make the learning fun. These books are great models to use in creating student-made books in the classroom, too.

Barreta, G. (2010). *Dear Deer: A book of homophones.* New York: Square Fish.

MacPherson, E. H. (1992). *A tale of tails.* Racine, WI: Merrigold Press.

Scheunemann, P. (2002). *Two kids got to go, too.* Minneapolis, MN: ABDO Publishing Co. (See also others in the homophone series.)

Terban, M. (2007). *Eight ate: A feast of homonym riddles.* New York: Sandpiper.

Demonstrate, Sort, Check, and Reflect

(See pages 77–79.) Prepare a set of words to use for teacher-directed modeling, such as for Sort 26: *Homophones with CVCe and CVVC Partners.*

1. Introduce the words in the sort and discuss any that are unfamiliar. Learn and practice unknown vocabulary words as described in the standard weekly routines on pages 71–72. Ask students to help you match the homophone partners so that you can compare their meanings and spellings. What do they notice about the words? (They sound the same but they have different spellings and meanings.) Point out that some of the words are spelled with the CVCe pattern and others are spelled with the CVVC pattern, but they all have the long-vowel sound. Put up the header cards for **CVVC tail** and **CVCe tale**. Discuss the meanings and spellings of these words. "Tail *spelled t-a-i-l means something an animal might have.* Tale *spelled t-a-l-e is a story that someone tells.* Tail *is a CVVC word, but* tale *is a CVCe word.*" Hold up one word card at a time and have students help you sort it into the CVCe or CVVC column. Always discuss the meaning of the word as you sort it. For example, hold up the word *made* and ask, "*Does* made *have the CVCe pattern, such as in* tale, *or the CVVC pattern, as in* tail? *Yes, it has the CVCe pattern, so we will put it under the word* tale." Continue with the students' help until all the words have been sorted. Let mistakes go for now.
2. When all the words have been sorted, have the students join in as you name them from top to bottom in the columns and check for any that need to be changed. "*Do all of these words have the CVCe pattern like* tale? *Do we need to move any?*" Now is the time to correct errors.
3. Repeat the sort with the group. This time, you may want to mix up the words, turn them face down in a deck, and let students take turns drawing a card and sorting it into the correct column. You can also simply pass out the cards and have the students take turns sorting them. Periodically check to see whether they remember the meaning of the word they are sorting. After sorting, model how to check by naming the words in each column and talking about how the words in each column are alike.
4. Give each student a copy of the sort for individual practice. Assign the task of cutting out the words and then sorting on their own in the same way they did in the group. Work with them to come up with small drawings that will help them recall the word meanings. On subsequent days, students should repeat the sorting activity several times. Involve the students in the other standard weekly routines and vocabulary activities described in this text and in *WTW EL* for the within word pattern stage.
5. Informally assess students on the vowel patterns and word meanings under study throughout the week. Observe students' accuracy and fluency in sorting and their knowledge of the English vocabulary. At the end of the week, call out some of the words you have been working with and ask students to think about whether the word is an example of the CVCe or CVVC pattern.

Extend

Provide numerous opportunities for students to read, write, and engage with the words in the sorts. Card games and silly stories are especially fun ways to review the words and talk about their spelling patterns. You may do a modeled writing activity for students in which you "accidentally" misspell a word (such as using *see* for *sea*) then discuss out loud your thinking and change the spelling. This think-aloud process will provide an example for your students as they do their own writing.

Completed Sorts 26 and 27 should look something like the following tables. Notes for the Spanish sort, Sort 28, follow.

Sort 26: Homophones with CVCe and CVVC Partners

(See page 77.)

CVVC tail	CVCe tale
pain	pane
road	rode
pail	pale
plain	plane
maid	made
soar	sore
mail	male
loan	lone
boar	bore
hair	hare
sail	sale

Sort 27: Homophones with *ee* and *ea* Partners

(See page 78.) This sort examines common homophone pairs with *ee* and *ea* vowel spellings. Follow the procedures listed in Demonstrate, Sort, Check, and Reflect and Extend outlined on page 73, but set up columns as with *ee* and *ea*. Prior to doing the sort, discuss these two ways to create the long *e* sound in words.

ee	ea
meet	meat
peek	peak
see	sea
heel	heal
steel	steal

ee	ea
need	knead
cheep	cheap
seem	seam
beet	beat
tee	tea
reed	read

Sort 28: Homophones in Spanish

(See page 79.) This sort builds on the Spanish language and literacy knowledge of bilingual students and demonstrates that homophones exist in languages other than English, too. In Spanish, two of the common ways that homophones appear are (1) when one word has an accent mark (*acento*) and another doesn't and (2) when a word has the same sound as another using different letters (*letras distintas*).

Conduct this sort in two steps: First, have students pair the homophones and discuss their meanings. A chart of the homophones and their meanings follows:

te	té	you, tea
el	él	the, he
has	haz	Conjugations of verbs *haber* (have) and *hacer* (make or do)
hola	ola	hello, wave
mi	mí	my, me
casa	caza	house, hunt
tubo	tuvo	tube, had
que	qué	that, what
tu	tú	your, you
hora	ora	hour, pray
si	sí	if, yes

After they pair the homophones, have students notice what makes the pairs different: Is it that one is accented and the other not, or do they use different letters to make the same sounds? Put out the header cards *acento/no acento*, meaning accent mark or not, and *letras distintas*, meaning different letters used to spell the same sound. Examine each homophone set and sort them as a pair into the correct column. Notice that common confusions for letters in

Spanish include the use of *b* or *v*, *s* or *z*, and *h* or no *h*. The completed sort should look something like the following:

acento/no acento		letras distintas	
te	té	has	haz
el	él	hola	ola
mi	mí	casa	caza
que	qué	tubo	tuvo
tu	tú	hora	ora
si	sí		

Spell Check: Homophone Spellings

(See page 80.) This spell check is a brief check of some of the homophone words presented in Sorts 26 and 27 using a word recognition format. Photocopy page 80 for all students you wish to participate in the assessment. Name each picture, then ask your students to circle the word under each picture that matches the correct spelling pattern. Following are the 12 words assessed:

1. deer　**2.** meat　**3.** tea
4. male　**5.** sail　**6.** hare
7. plane　**8.** pail　**9.** road
10. hair　**11.** sea　**12.** read

SORTS 26–28

SORT 26: Homophones with CVCe and CVVC Partners

CVVC tail	**CVCe tale**	mail
boar	made	pale
hare	road	plane
loan	male	sore
pane	lone	pain
plain	bore	sail
hair	soar	rode
pail	sale	maid

SORT 27: Homophones with *ee and ea* Partners

ee	**ea**	beat
need	meat	peak
sea	cheap	heel
seem	read	steal
peek	beet	tea
heal	tee	knead
meet	steel	see
reed	cheep	seam

SORT 28: Homophones in Spanish

acento/no acento	letras distintas	tuvo
te	que	sí
el	tu	mí
has	hora	ola
hola	té	haz
mi	si	tú
casa	qué	caza
tubo	él	ora

SPELL CHECK: Homophone Spellings

deer dear	meet meat	tee tea
mail male	sale sail	hare hair
plain plane	pale pail	road rode
hare hair	see sea	reed read

unit **7**

R-Influenced Vowel Patterns

Notes for the Teacher

The series of sorts in this unit investigates the spelling patterns for *r*-influenced (or *r*-controlled) vowels, such as in the words *her, sir, fur,* and *car*. For English learners from Spanish-speaking backgrounds, these patterns are difficult for two reasons. First, the /r/ sound as in *car* or *round* does not exist in Spanish, so it may be difficult to pronounce. Second, *r*-influenced words introduce another set of vowel sounds that need to be added to and differentiated from the multitude of sounds students have been asked to spell in their new language. Spanish has a much more limited set of sounds that the vowels may represent. Because of this ever-increasing complexity of spelling and sounds, it is important that instruction in the *r*-influenced vowel sounds is systematic and provides many opportunities for reinforcement and practice.

Regional variations may exist in the pronunciation of *r*-influenced vowels, so be flexible and listen to students' pronunciation as they sort. Do not overemphasize pronunciation with students; rather, encourage students to take steps toward the rolled *r* as best they can and as appropriate to your regional dialect.

Sort 29 in this chapter starts with long-vowel *r* words that retain the long sound of each vowel, such as in the words *square, spear, fire, store,* and *lure*. This first sort allows students to practice the /r/ sound in words that do not deviate from previous patterns. Sort 30 introduces the *r*-influenced sounds of *ar* as in *car, or* as in *corn,* and *er/ir/ur* as in *clerk, bird,* or *fur*. Students will need to use both sound and spelling pattern information to accurately sort words into these groups. Subsequent sorts then compare the *r*-influenced patterns for each vowel and ask students to identify the correct spelling pattern. The spell check in this unit provides a quick assessment of a selection of words containing *r*-influenced vowel sounds. If students have difficulty identifying the correct vowel spelling in these words, additional practice in this area may be necessary.

Standard Weekly Routines for Use With Sorts 29–35

Follow the series of procedures outlined on pages 26–28 with these sorts, including learning and practicing the vocabulary, working repeatedly with the sorts, providing extension activities, and conducting informal assessments. A spell check is included in this unit as a post-assessment. Because many words with *r*-influenced vowels may be spelled in a variety of ways, it is important to constantly assess students' use of spelling patterns. Regularly ask students to spell sample words as you work with them in small groups, and build in opportunities for students to reflect on what they are learning either orally or in writing following a sorting session.

It may also be helpful to have students illustrate specific words and label them to reinforce the correct spelling. Ongoing assessment helps you to catch misconceptions and provide instructional support when needed.

Literature Connection

Many texts for developing readers use words with a variety of *r*-influenced vowel patterns. Help students notice the many common words that use the patterns under study in this unit, such as *bird, horse, fire, barn, shark,* and *nurse.* Point out and discuss these words after students have read a book. Have students repeat common phrases that have *r*-influenced vowel sounds such as "There's music in the air!" Connect what students are reading to their word study learning through books such as the following.

Arnold, M. D. (2008). *Roar of a snore.* New York: Puffin.

Averril, E. (1983). *The fire cat.* New York: HarperCollins.

Borra, J. (2006). *The man who put words on birds.* London: Beautiful Books.

Hoff, S. (1985). *The horse in Harry's room.* New York: HarperCollins.

Martin, B., & Archambault, J. (1988). *Barn dance!* New York: Henry Holt and Co.

Thaler, M. (2009). *The school nurse from the Black Lagoon.* New York: Scholastic.

Thomson, S. L. (2006). *Amazing sharks!* New York: HarperCollins.

Demonstrate, Sort, Check, and Reflect

(See pages 89–95.) Prepare a set of words to use for teacher-directed modeling, such as for Sort 29: *Word Sort with Long-Vowel* R *Words.*

1. Introduce the words in the sort and discuss any that are unfamiliar. Learn and practice unknown vocabulary words as described in the standard weekly routines on pages 26–28. Ask students what they notice about the words (they all have a long-vowel sound with /r/ at the end). Point out that their word study will begin to focus on words that have an *r* connected to the vowel. In the first sort, the *r* is acting like most other consonants would, but in subsequent sorts the *r* may change the sound the vowel makes. Sort 29 is a simple introduction for students and asks them to sort the words by the long-vowel sound they hear. Put up the header cards and show students the five vowels. Say the words aloud and make sure students are able to pronounce them. If you like, have students discuss whether the long vowel is being created by a CVCe or CVVC pattern. Hold up one word card at a time and have students help you sort it into the column representing the vowel sound they hear. *"Which vowel sound do you hear in the word* stare? *Yes, it goes in the column with* square." Continue with the students' help until all the words have been sorted. Let mistakes go for now.

2. When all the words have been sorted, have the students join in as you name them from top to bottom in the columns and check for any that need to be changed. *"Do all of these words have the same long-vowel sound? Do we need to move any?"*

3. Repeat the sort with the group. This time, you may want to mix up the words, turn them face down in a deck, and let students take turns drawing a card and sorting it into the correct column. You can also simply pass out the cards and have the students take turns sorting them. After sorting, model how to check by naming the words in each column and talking about how the words in each column are alike. This is a good opportunity to informally assess how easily your students can distinguish the long-vowel sounds when they are connected to an /r/ sound.

4. Give each student a copy of the sort for individual practice. Assign the task of cutting out the words and then sorting on their own in the same way they did in the group. On subsequent days, students should repeat the sorting activity several times. Involve the students in the other standard weekly routines described in this text and in *WTW EL* for the within word pattern stage.

5. Informally assess students on the vowel patterns under study throughout the week. Observe students' accuracy and fluency in sorting and their knowledge of the English vocabulary. At the end of the week, call out some of the words you have been working with and ask students to think about the ways that *r* influences the vowel sounds in words.

Extend

Provide numerous opportunities for students to read, write, and engage with the words in the sorts. Board games, card games, and picture dictionaries are especially fun ways to review the words and discuss their spelling patterns. Note homophones that appear in the various sorts, such as *hair/hare*. Have students add these words to their homophone dictionaries or classroom charts. Reinforce vocabulary learning on a daily basis!

Completed sorts for this unit should look something like the following tables. Notes that are specific to individual sorts are included above each table of sorted words.

Sort 29: Word Sort with Long-Vowel *R* Words

(See page 89.)

ā square (square)	ē spear (spear)	ī fire (fire)	ō store (store)	ū lure (lure)
hair	year	tire	roar	pure
pair	near	wire	tore	cure
care	steer	hire	soar	
stare	deer		wore	
dare	gear			

Additional words: *bare, hare, fair, hear, fear, more, shore, oar, sure*

Sort 30: *R*-Influenced Word Sort

(See page 90.) This sort features words in which the vowel is altered by being followed by an *r*. Help students pronounce the vowel sounds and compare them to each other. Students may have little difficulty differentiating the *ar* and *or* sounds from the other words, but they will need to use visual recognition to sort the *er/ir/ur* words. Assure them that there is not a difference in sound in these words, despite the spelling difference. As always, make sure that students say the words aloud as they sort them into columns to ensure that they hear the sound differences that do or do not exist.

ar car (car)	er clerk (clerk)	ir bird (bird)	or corn (corn)	ur fur (fur)
bar	her	dirt	horn	turn
tar	term	sir	for	burn
star	per	girl	fork	curb
far	germ	stir		hurt

***Additional words:** part, start, dark, shark, term, herd, first, shirt, fork, north, storm, curl, church*

Sort 31: *R*-Influenced Patterns of *a*

(See page 91.) In this sort students compare two long-vowel patterns of *a* with the *r*-influenced sound, as in *car*. First sort by spelling pattern and then compare the sounds represented in each column.

ar car (car)	are square (square)	air chair (chair)
shark	fare	pair
mark	stare	hair
start	dare	stair
part	rare	fair
farm	hare	lair
far	care	
barn	share	
star	bare	

***Additional words:** yard, hard, harm, sharp, dark, scare, glare*

Sort 32: *R*-Influenced Patterns of *e*

(See page 92.) In this sort students compare two long-vowel patterns of *e* with the *r*-influenced sound, as in *clerk*. First sort by spelling pattern and then compare the sounds represented in each column.

er clerk (clerk)	ear spear (spear)	eer deer (deer)
her	fear	sheer
verb	hear	cheer
herb	year	steer
germ	dear	peer
herd	near	
perk	ear	
term	clear	
per	gear	
fern		

Additional words: *perch, stern, nerve, beard, tear, jeer, sneer*

Sort 33: *R*-Influenced Patterns of *i*

(See page 93.) In this sort students compare two long-vowel patterns of *i* with the *r*-influenced sound, as in *bird*. First sort by spelling pattern and then compare the sounds represented in each column.

ir bird (bird)	ire fire (fire)	ier pliers (pliers)
girl	tire	drier
third	hire	flier
twirl	spire	crier
dirt	wire	shier
thirst		
first		
skirt		
firm		
birth		
shirt		
whirl		
chirp		

Sort 34: *R*-Influenced Patterns of *u*

(See page 94.) In this sort students compare two long-vowel patterns of *u* with the *r*-influenced sound, as in *church.* First sort by spelling pattern and then compare the sounds represented in each column.

ur church (church)	ur_e nurse (nurse)	ure lure (lure)
surf	curse	pure
slurp	curve	cure
hurt	urge	sure
turn	purse	
purr	surge	
burp		
curb		
burst		
curl		
turf		
burn		

Additional words: *hurl, churn, blurt, splurge*

Sort 35: *R*-Influenced Patterns of *o*

(See page 95.) In this sort students compare two long-vowel patterns of *o* with the distinct *r*-influenced sounds, as in *corn* and *worm.* Notice that in *w* + *or* words the sound of *or* is /ər/ in words such as *work* and *world.* First sort by spelling pattern and then compare the sounds represented in each column. Give students time to discuss and compare the vowel sounds in each column. Ask students, "*In which two columns do the vowels make the same sound?* (Store *and* roar *columns.) What might help you remember how to pronounce or spell these words?*"

or corn (corn)	ore store (store)	oar roar (roar)	w + or worm (worm)
form	shore	board	work
north	more	oar	world
fork	chore	soar	

or corn (corn)	ore store (store)	oar roar (roar)	*w* + or worm (worm)
short	tore		
born	sore		
fort	score		
thorn			
storm			
cord			

***Additional words:** horn, pork, torn, dorm, bore, snore, boar, word, worth, worse*

Oddball Cards for *R*-Influenced Spelling Patterns

(See page 96.) These cards are provided so that you can selectively add them to make students' sorts more challenging once they are getting a good grasp on the regular patterns. Oddballs help students see that there are variations in the influence of vowels with *r* in the real-life world of words, and they help ensure that students are correctly pronouncing and differentiating their words as they sort.

pear	wear	bear
where	there	were
heart	their	heard
earth	learn	four
floor	door	pour
swear	your	are
war	court	fourth
quart		

Spell Check: *R*-Influenced Vowels

(See page 97.) This assessment is presented in a word-recognition format and checks for the correct spelling pattern of 20 words with *r*-influenced vowels. Photocopy page 97 for all students you wish to participate in the assessment. Name each picture, then ask your students to circle the word next to each picture that matches the correct spelling pattern. Following are the 20 words assessed:

1. fork	**2.** corn	**3.** tire
4. chair	**5.** horn	**6.** car
7. shirt	**8.** nurse	**9.** shark
10. girl	**11.** clerk	**12.** star
13. board	**14.** church	**15.** bird
16. deer	**17.** barn	**18.** world
19. thorn	**20.** four	

SORTS 29–35

SORT 29: Word Sort with Long-Vowel *R* Words

ā square	ē spear	ī fire
ō store	ū lure	hair
year	tire	pure
care	steer	hire
roar	wore	pair
cure	stare	tore
near	soar	deer
wire	gear	dare

SORT 30: *R*-Influenced Word Sort

ar car	**er** clerk	**or** corn
ur fur	**ir** bird	dirt
horn	turn	for
term	sir	her
burn	tar	curb
stir	girl	bar
far	fork	per
germ	star	hurt

SORT 31: *R*-Influenced Patterns of *a*

ar car	are square	air chair
fare	dare	start
shark	far	fair
stare	hare	bare
stair	barn	star
hair	share	pair
mark	lair	care
rare	part	farm

SORT 32: *R*-Influenced Patterns of *e*

er clerk	ear spear	eer deer
fear	her	steer
sheer	dear	hear
herd	cheer	herb
verb	ear	near
year	germ	peer
fern	clear	gear
per	perk	term

SORT 33: *R*-Influenced Patterns of *i*

ir bird	ire fire	ier pliers
tire	drier	third
flier	girl	hire
thirst	wire	twirl
first	skirt	dirt
crier	shier	whirl
firm	birth	chirp
shirt	spire	

SORT 34: *R-Influenced Patterns of u*

ur church	ure lure	ur_e nurse
turn	sure	surf
purr	curve	surge
burp	burn	purse
pure	turf	slurp
burst	urge	hurt
curse	curl	curb
cure		

SORT 35: *R*-Influenced Patterns of *o*

or corn	ore store	oar roar
w + or worm	form	board
more	work	shore
world	oar	thorn
soar	north	storm
fork	born	sore
short	tore	cord
chore	fort	score

Oddball Cards for *R*-Influenced Vowels

pear	wear	bear
where	there	were
heart	their	heard
earth	learn	four
floor	door	pour
swear	your	are

SPELL CHECK: ***R*-Influenced Vowels**

1. foark fork forek	**2.** corne coarn corn
3. tire tier tyer	**4.** chear chair chare
5. hoarn horn hoern	**6.** carr caur car
7. shirt shert shurt	**8.** nerse nearse nurse
9. shrak shark sheark	**10.** girl gril gerl
11. clurk clerk clirk	**12.** ster stair star
13. bord board boord	**14.** cherch chirch church
15. bird berd burd	**16.** dear dere deer
17. baren barn barne	**18.** werld world world
19. thoarn thorne thorn	**20.** for four fore

unit

8 Diphthongs and Other Vowel Patterns

Notes for the Teacher

The series of sorts in this unit is designed for students at the late within word pattern stage. These sorts extend students' knowledge of vowel patterns in English, this time by learning about diphthongs—two vowels that glide into each other within the same syllable, such as in the word *cloud,* and ambiguous vowels, such as in the words *raw*, *caught*, or *talk*. Diphthongs may be relatively easy for Spanish-speaking students because the sounds of both vowels can be distinguished, and Spanish contains many diphthongs (e.g., *voy, oigo, causa, playa*). Ambiguous vowels, on the other hand, can be tremendously difficult. Not only will students need to come to recognize a variety of possible patterns for spelling the ambiguous vowel sounds in words, they may have difficulty distinguishing the slight differences in pronunciation that could support them in this process. Although there are only five sorts in this unit, take your time presenting and practicing them. Listen to students as they say the words aloud and assess whether their pronunciation is influencing pattern recognition. When students experience confusion, take the time to repeat a sort, review key words, and work toward mastery. Reinforce the spelling patterns of common ambiguous vowel words by using them in reading and writing activities outside of word study time.

Regional variations may exist in the pronunciation of ambiguous vowels, so be flexible and listen to students' pronunciation as they sort. As Spanish-speaking students encounter new words in their reading and word study, they may attempt to pronounce each sound in a vowel pattern, such as pronouncing *pause* as "pah-oose." Do not overemphasize pronunciation with students; rather, guide students to see the ambiguous vowel sound as one unit and reinforce the pattern by working with rhyming words that have the same sound (e.g., *paw, saw, law, thaw*). Using a supportive manner, help students to pronounce the words as best they can and as appropriate to your regional dialect.

Sort 36 in this unit is a word sort that compares the diphthongs *oi*/*oy* and *ou*/*ow*. Students will first differentiate the words by spelling pattern and then see that *oi* and *oy* (and *ou* and *ow*) are two ways of spelling the same sounds. This word study lesson then guides students to notice that the *oy* and *ow* patterns usually occur at the end of a word. Sort 37 is a word and picture sort that compares words by sounds: /oy/, /ow/, or long *o*. This sort may also be broken down into two sorts, each sort comparing one of the diphthongs with the long-vowel *o* sound, if students are not easily grasping the distinctions.

Sort 38 introduces the vowel patterns represented by *oo,* such as in the words *tooth* and *hook.* Subsequent sorts then compare ambiguous vowel sounds that are close in sound but vary in spelling, such as in the words *clock, claw,* and *sauce* or *salt, wall,* and *thought*. The spell check in this unit provides a quick assessment of diphthongs and other vowel patterns. If students have difficulty identifying the correct vowel spelling in these words, additional practice in one or more of the patterns may be necessary.

Standard Weekly Routines for Use with Sorts 36–40

Follow the series of instructional procedures outlined on pages 26–28 with these sorts, including learning and practicing the vocabulary, working repeatedly with the sorts, providing extension activities, and conducting informal assessments. A spell check is included in this unit as a post-assessment. Because many words with ambiguous vowel sounds may be spelled in a variety of ways, it is important to constantly assess students' use of spelling patterns. Regularly ask students to spell sample words as you work with them in small groups, and build in opportunities for students to reflect orally or in writing following a sorting session. It may also be helpful to have students illustrate specific words or a sentence that includes the word to reinforce its spelling. Ongoing assessment is one way of preventing misconceptions and planning additional support as needed.

Literature Connection

Many texts for developing readers use words with diphthongs and other vowel patterns. Help students notice the many common words that use the patterns under study in this unit so that the correct spelling patterns become more familiar and accessible to them. Highlight some of the diphthong and other vowel pattern words that are used in the texts you read together, such as *boy*, *mouth*, *tooth*, *book*, and *saw*. The following books provide examples of many diphthong and other vowel words to notice and discuss.

Ada, A. F. (1994). *The gold coin*. New York: Aladdin Paperbacks.

Bagert, B. (2007). *Shout! Little poems that roar.* New York: Dial.

Beeler, S. (2001). *Throw your tooth from the roof: Tooth traditions from around the world.* New York: Sandpiper.

dePaola, T. (1984). *The cloud book*. New York: Holiday House.

Hoberman, M. (2003). *And to think that we thought that we'd never be friends.* Decorah, IA: Dragonfly Books.

Hooks, B. (2008). *Grump groan growl.* New York: Hyperion Books.

Hooks, W. (1990). *Moss gown.* New York: Sandpiper.

Jeffers, O. (2007). *The incredible book-eating boy.* New York: Philomel.

Oram, H. (2000). *Little brother and the cough.* London: Frances Lincoln.

Staake, B. (2011). *Look! A book!* New York: Little, Brown Books for Young Readers.

Weeks, S. (2002). *Mrs. McNosh hangs up her wash.* New York: HarperCollins.

Demonstrate, Sort, Check, and Reflect

(See page 105.) Prepare a set of words to use for teacher-directed modeling, such as for Sort 36: *Word Sort with Diphthongs.*

1. Introduce the words in the sort and discuss any that are unfamiliar. Learn and practice unknown vocabulary words as described in the standard weekly routines on pages 26–28. Ask students what they notice about the words (some have the "oi" sound and some have the "ou" sound). Point out that in all of the words the vowel sounds "slide" from one part of the mouth to another, as in the word *spoil* where the first part of the vowel sound is like a long *o* and then the mouth moves to more like a long *e* sound. Have students say *spoil* slowly so that they can hear and feel this transition. In Part 1 of Sort 36, students are asked to discriminate between words that have the /oy/ sound and those that have the /ow/ sound. In your first sort, create two columns, one with the header cards **oi coin** and **oy boy**, and the other with the header cards **ou mouth** and **ow cow**. Help students practice comparing the words *coin* and *boy* to make sure they hear that both patterns represent the same sound. Do the same with the words *mouth* and *cow*. Have students discuss the similarities and differences in how the /oy/ and /ow/ sounds are being represented. Next, begin to work through each of the sorting words, saying each aloud and deciding whether it belongs in the boy/coin column or the mouth/cow column. Hold up one word card at a time and have students help you sort it into the column representing the vowel sound they hear. "*Which vowel sound do you hear in the word* boil? *Yes, it goes in the column with* boy *and* coin." Continue with the students' help until all the words have been sorted. Let mistakes go for now.
2. When all the words have been sorted, have the students join in as you name them from top to bottom in the columns and check for any that need to be changed. "*Do all of these words have the same vowel sound? Do we need to move any?*"
3. Repeat the sort with the group. This time, you may want to mix up the words, turn them face down in a deck, and let students take turns drawing a card and sorting it into the correct column. You can also simply pass out the cards and have the children take turns sorting them. After sorting, model how to check by naming the words in each column and talking about how the words in each column are alike. This is a good opportunity to informally assess how easily your students can distinguish the vowel sounds of the diphthongs /oy/ and /ow/.
4. Once you are confident that students are able to differentiate the vowel sounds in these words you can move to Part 2 of the sort: identifying when /oy/ is spelled using *oy* or *oi* and when /ow/ is spelled using *ow* or *ou*. After completing the sort as described in step 1 above, direct students' attention to the /oy/ words. Point out that there are two header cards in this group—**oy boy** and **oi coin**. Put each of these cards at the top of a column and ask students to look at the spelling of the words in that group. Which words belong under *boy* and which belong below *coin*? "*Should* boil *be placed under* boy *or* coin? *Yes, it goes with* coin *because it is spelled with* oi *not* oy." Continue with the students' help until all the words have been sorted. What do your students notice about when /oy/ is spelled with *oi* and when it is spelled with *oy*? (Usually *oy* is used at the end of a word, and *oi* is used in the middle of a word.) Next, do the same for the /ow/ words, separating the sorting words into those that belong with **ow cow** or **ou mouth**. Discuss when /ow/ is represented by *ou* and when it is represented by *ow*. Do students perceive a similar pattern? The completed sort should look something like the Sort 36 table in the following section.
5. Give each student a copy of the sort for individual practice. Assign the task of cutting out the words and then sorting on their own in the same way they did in the group. First ask students to sort their words by comparing the sounds of /oy/ and /ow/. When they can do this easily, ask students to subdivide words based on their spelling pattern. On subsequent days students should repeat the sorting activity several times. Involve the students in the other standard weekly routines described in this text and in *WTW EL* for the within word pattern stage.
6. Informally assess students on the vowel patterns under study throughout the week. Observe students' accuracy and fluency in sorting and their knowledge of the English vocabulary. At the end of the week, call out some of the words you have been working with and ask students to think about how some vowel sounds slide from one sound to another, such as in /oy/ and /ow/, and how their spellings may be represented differently depending on their location within a word.

Extend

Provide numerous opportunities for students to read, write, and engage with the words in the sorts. Board games, card games, and picture dictionaries are especially fun ways to review the words and discuss their spelling patterns. Once students have internalized the spelling patterns in these sorts, consider investigating additional words with diphthongs that are part of compound words, such as *toybox*, *boyfriend*, *joyful*, or *cowhand*. Why might these words retain their original spelling even though the /oy/ or /ow/ sound is no longer at the end of a word?

Completed sorts for this unit should look something like the following tables. Notes that are specific to individual sorts are included above each table of sorted words.

Sort 36: Word Sort with Diphthongs

(See page 105.)

/oy/ sound		/ow/ sound	
oi coin (coin)	**oy boy (boy)**	**ou mouth (mouth)**	**ow cow (cow)**
oil	joy	shout	plow
soil	toy	found	how
boil		south	town
spoil		pound	now
join		count	gown
voice			owl
			growl

Additional words: *soy, ploy, point, foil, noise, cloud, out, couch, round, drown, down, clown*

Sort 37: Word Sort with Long *o*, *oi/oy*, and *ou/ow*

(See page 106.) This sort compares words that have the /oy/ sound, the /ow/ sound, and the long sound of *o*. Invite students to listen carefully to identify the vowel sounds within each word before sorting. Pictures are included in this sort to ensure that students are listening carefully to the vowel sounds in the words and are not simply scanning for the spelling pattern.

ō bone (bone)	oi, oy boy (boy)	ou, ow cow (cow)
(road)	(coin)	(owl)
soak	(toy)	now

ō bone (bone)	oi, oy boy (boy)	ou, ow cow (cow)
(goat)	oil	south
(soap)	(join)	(mouth)
loan	boil	town
wrote	spoil	(shout)
hope		
those		
coat		

Additional words: *whole, cone, home, stone, vote, load, boat, croak, joy, soy, point, voice, noise, moist, how, frown, count, shout, scout*

Sort 38: Word Sort with o͞o and o͝o

(See page 107.) In this sort students compare two vowel sounds that are represented with o͞o, such as in *tooth* or o͝o such as in *hook or would.* The vowel sound in *tooth* should not be especially difficult for Spanish-speaking students because it is similar to the long *u* sound that is present in Spanish. The vowel sound in *book,* however, does not exist in Spanish and may be difficult for students to distinguish and pronounce. Remember to help students with their pronunciation, but do not fixate on it. If differentiating these two vowel sounds is beyond students' perceptual abilities at the current moment, help by pronouncing words for them and having them watch your mouth as you say the words. Do not worry if this sort needs extra scaffolding; at the least it will be a first step for students on the road to distinguishing some of the subtle vowels sounds and patterns that they will continue to engage with for years to come.

o͞o tooth (tooth)	o͝o hook (hook)
room	would
proof	should
stool	wood
(root)	(crook)
(hoop)	stood
root	(hood)
cool	could
gloom	hood
(spoon)	
fool	
noon	

o͞o tooth (tooth)	o͝o hook (hook)
hoop	
(stool)	
scoop	

Additional words: *good, food, mood, look, book, groom, zoom, doom, spook, wool*

Sort 39: Word Sort with Ambiguous Vowel Sounds, Part 1

(See page 108.) In this sort students compare vowel patterns whose sounds closely resemble each other, as in the words *clock, claw,* and *sauce.* Have students sort the words by their spelling pattern and then compare and contrast the pronunciation of these vowel sounds that exist in your region.

ŏ clock (clock)	aw claw (claw)	au sauce (sauce)
cloth	draw	pause
long	dawn	haul
soft	raw	fault
toss	thaw	cause
frost	yawn	
	crawl	
	law	
	straw	
	saw	
	paw	
	hawk	

Additional words: *block, trot, chop, drop, shawl, lawn, jaw, haunt, cause, launch*

Sort 40: Word Sort with Ambiguous Vowel Sounds, Part 2

(See page 109.) In this sort students continue to compare vowel patterns whose sounds closely resemble each other, as in the words *salt, water,* and *thought.* Because there are a number of ways that these vowel sounds can be spelled, it is difficult for the speller to know which form to use. As in previous sorts, guide students to sort by spelling pattern and then examine the sound similarities and differences that exist in your regional pronunciations.

al salt (salt)	w + a water (water)	ough thought (thought)
halt	wasp	cough
calm	wash	ought
tall	watt	bought
bald	want	brought
mall	wall	fought
palm	swap	
talk	watch	
small	wand	

Additional words: *walk, warm, stalk, chalk, ball, fall, tall, sought*

Oddball Cards for Diphthongs and Other Vowel Patterns

(See page 110.) These cards are provided so that you can selectively add them to make students' sorts more challenging. Oddballs help students see that not all words with diphthongs or the other vowels studied in this section have consistent sound-spelling relationships and help ensure that students are correctly pronouncing and reading the words as they sort.

Spell Check: Diphthongs and Other Vowel Patterns

(See page 111.) This assessment is presented in a word-recognition format and checks for the correct spelling pattern of 20 words with diphthongs and ambiguous vowels. Photocopy page 111 for all students you wish to participate in the assessment. Name each picture, then ask your students to circle the word next to the picture that matches the correct spelling pattern. Following are the 18 words assessed:

1. claw
2. bald
3. root
4. mouth
5. hook
6. tooth
7. spoon
8. boy
9. owl
10. paw
11. coin
12. hood
13. watch
14. toy
15. palm
16. stool
17. cow
18. sauce
19. wash
20. crook

SORTS 36–40

SORT 36: Word Sort with Diphthongs

oi coin	oy boy	ou mouth
ow cow	oil	joy
toy	shout	plow
found	how	soil
boil	south	town
pound	gown	now
owl	spoil	count
voice	growl	join

SORT 37: Word Sort with Long *o, oi/oy,* and *ou/ow*

bōne	oi, oy boy	ou, ow cow
	oil	
now		soak
south	boil	
	spoil	loan
hope		
those		wrote
	coat	town

SORT 38: Word Sort with $\bar{oo}$ and $\breve{oo}$

$\bar{oo}$ tooth	$\breve{oo}$ hook	room
wood	cool	would
	hood	proof
	noon	should
fool	could	stool
stood	scoop	
hoop		
	gloom	root

SORT 39: Word Sort with Ambiguous Vowel Sounds, Part 1

ŏ clock	aw claw	au sauce
dawn	cloth	draw
fault	cause	pause
frost	crawl	long
paw	law	haul
saw	gnaw	straw
hawk	toss	yawn
thaw	raw	soft

SORT 40: Word Sort with Ambiguous Vowel Sounds, Part 2

al salt	w + a water	ough thought
cough	want	tall
mall	wall	wash
wasp	ought	halt
talk	watch	fought
small	wand	calm
bought	bald	watt
swap	brought	palm

Oddball Cards for Diphthongs and Other Vowel Patterns

would	could	should
laugh	though	through
tough	rough	brought
thought	blood	young
you	cough	ought
bought		

SPELL CHECK: Diphthongs and Other Vowel Patterns

1. clau claw clough	**2.** bald bauld bowld
3. rout rut root	**4.** mowth mooth mouth
5. hoke hook huik	**6.** tooth tuthe tuith
7. spon spoon spune	**8.** boye boi boy
9. oul owel owl	**10.** pa paw paow
11. coyn coin coun	**12.** houd hoid hood
13. wautch walch watch	**14.** toy toye toiy
15. palm pam paum	**16.** stule stuwel stool
17. cough cow cowe	**18.** sause salse sauce
19. walsh waush wash	**20.** crook cruk cruck

unit

9

Beginning and Ending Complex Consonants and Consonant Clusters

Notes for the Teacher

The series of sorts in this unit is designed for students at the late within word pattern stage. In this unit we take a break from vowel patterns to focus on the complex clusters of consonants that begin or end single-syllable words. Examples of these consonant clusters include those that begin the words *knife, write, gnat, spring, street, scrape, squat, three,* and *shrink*. Sorts 41–43 provide opportunities for students to dig deeply into the sounds and spellings of these complex beginning sounds, and apply their learning to a variety of words that represent short, long, and other vowel patterns. The first spell check in this unit, "Beginning Complex Consonant Clusters," provides a brief assessment of students' skill in applying these beginning complex consonant clusters in their spelling. Following this section, in Sorts 44–45, students investigate two complex ending sounds: *dge* versus *ge*, and *tch* versus *ch* as in the words *bridge, page, switch,* and *beach*. The spell check "Ending Complex Consonant Clusters" is provided to assess students' use of these complex ending consonant clusters, and may be administered as either a pre- or post-test.

Students from Spanish-speaking backgrounds may find many of the complex consonant clusters featured in this section of sorts tricky. In Spanish some consonant blends are used, but not in groups of three letters. Additionally, Spanish does not use *s*-blends such as in the words *stamp* or *scale*. In Spanish these words would have a vowel added so that the blend would break one syllable into two (e.g., *estampa, escala*). Imagine how unlike Spanish a word such as *scratch* would seem. In a related issue, there are few letters that are permitted to end words in Spanish (the vowels plus *d, l, n, r, s, z*), and certainly consonant clusters at the end of words would not occur. For these reasons, Spanish-speaking students may find the spelling patterns in these sorts particularly challenging. Remember to provide support for students as they say the words, identify the clusters that represent the sounds, and analyze which letters are needed to accurately spell the representative words.

Many of the words in this unit not only grab the reader's attention—they are also tricky on the tongue. Think of the words *squish, shrank,* or *sprout* for example. As you explore these words consider chanting phrases or reading books that include these interesting words (e.g., "squish, squish, squish went the boots in the mud"). Provide many opportunities for students to use the words in their writing or in talk bubbles for illustrations (e.g., *shriek, scram, gnaw, wreck*). Knowing that these words are difficult may help you slow down your instruction, listen to students' oral confusions, and note how their developmental spelling is (or isn't) accurately representing the many sounds within each word.

Sort 41 in this unit introduces words with silent beginning consonants, such as *knew, wrong,* and *gnaw*. Silent letters are challenging for young writers, so it may prove helpful to have many opportunities to sort and re-sort these common words and gain familiarity with their spelling patterns. Sorts 42 and 43 ask students to differentiate the beginning sound and spelling patterns of words with triple blends or a digraph/blend combination. As noted previously, these words can be difficult for English learners to dissect, pronounce, and spell. Sorts 44 and 45 examine the vowel patterns that determine whether a word will need to be spelled with *tch* or *ch* and *dge* or *ge*, depending on whether the word has a long-vowel, short-vowel, or other vowel sound. Once these types of complex single-syllable words are mastered, students will be nearing the end of the within word pattern stage and ready to focus on the meaning layer of orthographic development.

Standard Weekly Routines for Use with Sorts 41–45

Follow the series of instructional procedures outlined on pages 26–28 with these sorts, including learning and practicing the vocabulary, working repeatedly with the sorts, providing extension activities, and conducting informal assessments. The "Beginning Complex Consonant Clusters" and "Ending Complex Consonant Clusters" spell checks are included in this unit as post-assessments. When you cover the beginning consonant clusters in these sorts, it will be important to help students match what they see in a word with how it is pronounced. For example, in the word *shrub* the sounds /sh/, /r/, /u/, and /b/ need to be represented in print and pronounced. For the final *–dge/ge* and *–tch/ch*, however, the focus will be not be on hearing differences in the consonant sounds, but rather on ascertaining how the placement of consonants controls the vowel sound. It will be important for students to receive explicit guidance and support as they tackle these complex features within single-syllable words. Frequent assessment is one way of preventing misconceptions. Use the results of your informal assessments to plan additional support as needed.

Literature Connection

Many poems, comic books, and other texts for developing readers use words with complex consonants. Help students thrill to the many common words that contain the clusters of letters under study in this chapter so that they can then use these spelling patterns in their own writing. Emphasize some of the interesting words that are used in the texts you read together, such as *scream*, *squish*, *gnaw*, *sprout*, *wreck*, and *threat*. The following books highlight a few examples of the many words with complex consonant clusters that you and your students can discover and enjoy.

Berenstain, S., & Berenstain, J. (1998). *The Berenstain Bears scream their heads off.* New York: Scholastic.

Brown, D..(1995). *Ruth Law thrills a nation.* Boston: Houghton Mifflin.

Doudna, K. (2002). *Do not squash the squash!* Minneapolis, MN: ABDO Sandcastle.

Joyce, W. (1987). *George shrinks.* New York: HarperCollins.

Mitton, T. (2009). *Gnash, gnaw, dinosaur!* New York: Kingfisher.

Nuzzolo, D. (2007). *Shrimp.* Mankato, MN: Capstone Press.

Pulver, R. (2010). *Silent letters loud and clear.* New York: Holiday House.

Reisner, M., & Ostrow, K. (2004). *Camp SpongeBob.* New York: Simon & Schuster.

Wortche, A. (2011). *Rosie Sprout's time to shine.* New York: Knopf Books for Young Readers.

Zimmer, T. V. (2005). *Sketches from a spy tree.* New York: Clarion Books.

Demonstrate, Sort, Check, and Reflect

(See pages 119–124.) Prepare a set of words to use for teacher-directed modeling, such as for Sort 41: *Word Sort with Silent Beginning Consonants* kn, wr, *and* gn.

1. Introduce the words in the sort and discuss any that are unfamiliar. Learn and practice unknown vocabulary words as described in the standard weekly routines on pages 26–28. Ask students what they notice about the words (they begin with two consonants, but one is silent). Point out that all of the words begin with *kn, wr,* or *gn*. Say the words aloud together and emphasize that each beginning pair represents only one sound. Since there is only one sound clue to the spelling of the beginning of the word, students will need to use their familiarity with the word to spell it correctly with an additional silent letter. Have students discuss the ways that /n/ might be spelled at the beginning of a word. Brainstorm a few words together, such as *night, next, know,* or *knee*. Point out that using *gn* to represent this sound is not very common, but that it is important for advancing readers to know about this spelling pattern. Spend a minute discussing *wr* as a spelling unit. What other ways might /r/ be spelled? Next, work through each of the sorting words, saying each aloud and deciding whether it belongs in the *kn* knife column, the *wr* wrist column, or the *gn* gnat column. Hold up one word card at a time and ask students to say the word and help you sort it into the column representing the initial consonant pair it contains. "*What initial consonant pair do you see in* kneel? *Yes, it goes in the column with* knife." Continue with the students' help until all the words have been sorted. Let mistakes go for now.
2. When all the words have been sorted, have the students join in as you name the words from top to bottom in the columns and check for any that need to be changed. "*Do all of these words have the same beginning consonant pairs? Do we need to move any?*"
3. Repeat the sort with the group. This time, you may want to mix up the words, turn them face down in a deck, and let students take turns drawing a card and sorting it in the correct column. You can also simply pass out the cards and have the students take turns sorting them. After sorting, model how to check by naming the words in each column and talking about how the words in each column are alike. It is very important that students say the words aloud as they sort to make the sound/spelling pattern connection.
4. Give each student a copy of the sort for individual practice. Assign the task of cutting out the words and then sorting on their own in the same way they did in the group. Ask students to sort their words by comparing the beginning consonants *kn, wr,* and *gn*. On subsequent days students should repeat the sorting activity several times. Involve the students in the other standard weekly routines described in this text and in *WTW EL* for the within word pattern stage.
5. Informally assess students on the beginning consonant patterns under study throughout the week. Observe students' accuracy and fluency in sorting, their pronunciation of the words, and their knowledge of the English vocabulary. At the end of the week, call out some of the words you have been working with and ask students to think about the silent letters that need to be included when these words are written.

Extend

Provide numerous opportunities for students to read, write, and engage with the words in the sorts. Board games, card games, and picture dictionaries are especially fun ways to review the words and discuss their spelling patterns. Create a classroom chart or a page in students' word study notebooks to add other words they find that begin with *kn, wr,* or *gn*. Which group of words seems to be the most and least common? Compare words that create homophones, such as *no* and *know* or *write* and *right*. What other homophones may be found with *kn, wr,* or *gn* words?

Completed sorts for this unit should look something like in the following tables. Notes that are specific to individual sorts are included above each table of sorted words.

Sort 41: Word Sort with Silent Beginning Consonants *kn, wr, and gn*

(See page 119.)

kn knife (knife)	wr wrist (wrist)	gn gnat (gnat)
know	wreath	gnaw
known	wrap	gnash
knight	wrath	gnarl
knob	wreck	gnome
knot	wrong	
knit	wrote	
kneel	write	
knock		
knew		
knee		

Additional words: *knack, knelt, knead, wring, wren, writhe, gnu*

Sort 42: Word Sort with Triple R-Blends *spr, str, and scr*

(See page 120.) In this sort students compare words that begin with three consonants featuring an *s*-blend followed by an *r*. Students have an opportunity to not only differentiate and master these complex sounds, but also put into practice many of the vowel patterns they have previously studied.

spr spring (spring)	str street (street)	scr screw (screw)
spread	strap	scrape
spray	strong	scram
sprain	strict	scratch
sprawl	stripe	scream

spr spring (spring)	str street (street)	scr screw (screw)
sprout	stray	screen
spree	straight	scrap
sprint	straw	
	stream	

***Additional words:** spur, sprite, spruce, strain, strand, strange, strength, stress, stretch, strike, string, struck, screech, scrawl, scribe, script*

Sort 43: Word Sort with *squ, thr,* and *shr*

(See page 121.) In this sort students compare words that begin with the *squ*, *thr*, and *shr* sounds.

squ square (square)	thr three (three)	shr shrub (shrub)
squirt	throw	shred
squash	through	shrimp
squeak	thread	shrink
squirm	thrill	shrill
squish	threw	shrank
squeeze	threat	shriek
squint	throne	
squad		

***Additional words:** squawk, squat, squeal, squid, throat, thrown, thrash, thrift, shrunk, shrew, shrewd, shrug*

Spell Check: Beginning Complex Consonant Clusters

(See page 122.) This assessment evaluates students' understanding of the complex beginning sound clusters contained in Sorts 41–43. Name each picture; then ask your students to think about the string of consonants that begin each of the words and write the spelling of the word on the lines provided. Pictures are provided to reinforce students' understanding of the words you are saying. Following are the 18 words assessed:

1. square	**2.** knife	**3.** three
4. wrist	**5.** shrub	**6.** gnat
7. knob	**8.** spring	**9.** gnome
10. thread	**11.** stripe	**12.** shrimp
13. street	**14.** knee	**15.** sprint
16. screw	**17.** sprout	**18.** wreath

Sort 44: Word Sort with Endings *dge* and *ge*

(See page 123.) In this sort students compare single-syllable words that end with the /j/ sound, as in *bridge, page* and *sponge.* The trick to the spelling pattern *dge* or *ge* is the vowel sound that precedes it. Short-vowel words are usually spelled with *dge*, such as in the word *bridge;* long vowels, ambiguous vowels, and the letters *r, l,* and *n* precede the *ge* spelling. As you lead this activity, guide students to sort by short-vowel sound, long-vowel sound, or vowel + *r, l,* or *n.*

dge bridge (bridge)	ge page (page)	r, l, n + ge sponge (sponge)
wedge	cage	large
smudge	age	range
judge	huge	change
trudge	stage	gorge
edge		strange
dodge		urge
		bulge
		hinge
		charge
		merge
		twinge

Additional words: *badge, ridge, fudge, lodge, wage, surge, plunge, lunge*

Sort 45: Word Sort with Endings *tch* and *ch*

(See page 124.) This sort follows the same principle illustrated in Sort 44. In this sort students compare single-syllable words that end with the /ch/ sound, as in *switch, beach,* and *lunch.* The trick to the spelling pattern *tch* or *ch* is, once again, the vowel sound that precedes it. Short-vowel words are usually spelled with *tch*, such as in the word *switch;* long vowels, ambiguous vowels, and the letters *r*, *l*, and *n* precede the *ch* spelling. As you lead this activity, guide students to sort by short-vowel sound, long-vowel sound, or vowel + *r*, *l*, or *n*.

tch switch (switch)	ch beach (beach)	r, l, n + ch lunch (lunch)
match	roach	bench
witch	reach	arch
pitch	speech	pinch
fetch	screech	branch
sketch	coach	march
catch		torch
		crunch
		church
		porch
		inch

***Additional words:** itch, batch, blotch, crutch, ditch, latch, patch, peach, teach, clench, search, perch*

Spell Check: Ending Complex Consonant Clusters

(See page 125.) This assessment is a brief check of some of the words with complex ending consonants presented in Sorts 44 and 45 using a word recognition format. Photocopy page 125 for all students you wish to participate in the assessment. Name each picture; then ask the students to circle the word under each picture that matches the correct spelling pattern. Following are the 12 words assessed:

1. switch	**2.** branch	**3.** beach
4. bridge	**5.** church	**6.** stage
7. lunch	**8.** page	**9.** peach
10. arch	**11.** match	**12.** sponge

SORTS 41–45

SORT 41: Word Sort with Silent Beginning Consonants *kn, wr,* and *gn*

kn knife	wr wrist	gn gnat
write	gnaw	wrote
known	wrap	gnash
wrath	knot	know
knob	wreck	knee
gnarl	kneel	gnome
knit	knock	wreath
wrong	knew	knight

SORT 42: Word Sort with Triple R-Blends *spr, str,* and *scr*

spr spring	str street	scr screw
sprout	scrape	strap
scram	straight	spread
stripe	sprain	scrap
sprint	stray	strong
scratch	stream	spray
spree	scream	strict
straw	sprawl	screen

SORT 43: Word Sort with *squ, thr,* and *shr*

squ square	thr three	shr shrub
throw	squeak	thrill
shrink	threat	squish
squash	shred	shriek
shrill	throne	squeeze
through	shrimp	squint
shrank	squirm	threw
squirt	thread	squad

SPELL CHECK: *Beginning Complex Consonant Clusters*

Name ____________________

kn wr gn spr str scr squ thr shr

1.	2.
3.	4.
5.	6.
7.	8.
9.	10.
11.	12.
13.	14.
15.	16.
17.	18.

SORT 44: Word Sort with Endings *dge* and *ge*

dge bridge	**ge** page	**r, l, n + *ge*** sponge
edge	large	cage
age	stage	judge
gorge	dodge	bulge
strange	huge	hinge
urge	change	smudge
trudge	range	merge
twinge	wedge	charge

SORT 45: Word Sort with Endings *tch* and *ch*

tch switch	ch beach	r, l, n + ch lunch
reach	match	torch
branch	bench	roach
catch	arch	church
march	screech	porch
speech	witch	inch
crunch	coach	pitch
sketch	pinch	fetch

SPELL CHECK: Ending Complex Consonant Clusters

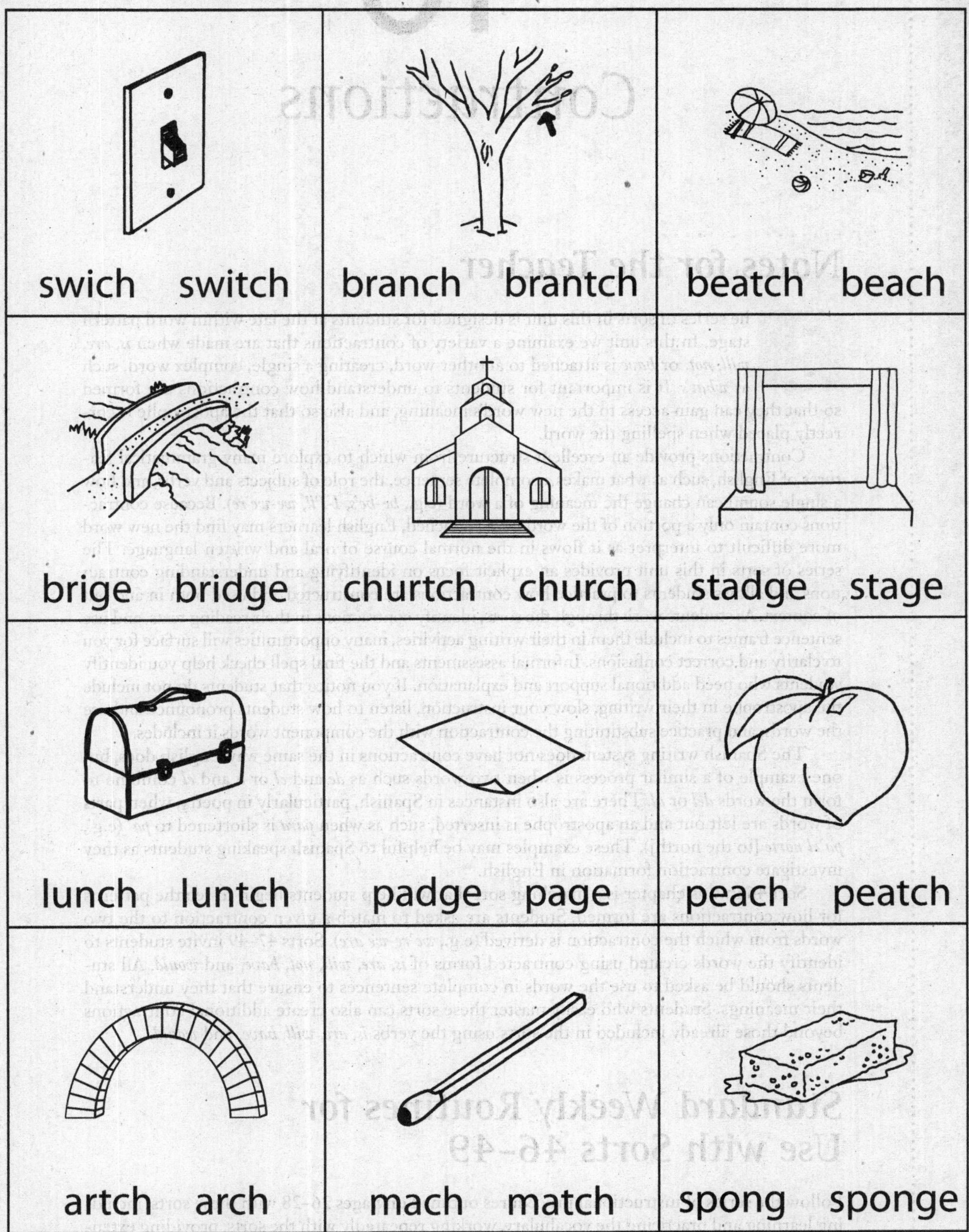

unit 10

Contractions

Notes for the Teacher

The series of sorts in this unit is designed for students at the late within word pattern stage. In this unit we examine a variety of contractions that are made when *is*, *are*, *will*, *not*, or *have* is attached to another word, creating a single, complex word, such as *what's*. It is important for students to understand how contractions are formed so that they can gain access to the new word's meaning, and also so that the apostrophe is correctly placed when spelling the word.

Contractions provide an excellent structure from which to explore many grammatical features of English, such as what makes a complete sentence, the role of subjects and verbs, and how a single sound can change the meaning of a word (e.g., *he-he's*, *I-I'll*, *we-we're*). Because contractions contain only a portion of the word being attached, English learners may find the new word more difficult to interpret as it flows in the normal course of oral and written language. The series of sorts in this unit provides an explicit focus on identifying and understanding contractions and allows students to practice how contractions are constructed and used both in and out of context. As students work through the sorts, identify contractions in their reading texts, and use sentence frames to include them in their writing activities, many opportunities will surface for you to clarify and correct confusions. Informal assessments and the final spell check help you identify students who need additional support and explanation. If you notice that students do not include the apostrophe in their writing, slow your instruction, listen to how students pronounce and use the words, and practice substituting the contraction with the component words it includes.

The Spanish writing system does not have contractions in the same way English does, but one example of a similar process is when two words such as *de* and *el* or *a* and *el* combine to form the words *del* or *al*. There are also instances in Spanish, particularly in poetry, when parts of words are left out and an apostrophe is inserted, such as when *para* is shortened to *pa'* (e.g., *pa'el norte* [to the north]). These examples may be helpful to Spanish speaking students as they investigate contraction formation in English.

Sort 46 in this chapter is a matching sort that will help students begin to see the patterns for how contractions are formed. Students are asked to match a given contraction to the two words from which the contraction is derived (e.g., *we're-we are*). Sorts 47–49 invite students to identify the words created using contracted forms of *is*, *are*, *will*, *not*, *have*, and *would*. All students should be asked to use the words in complete sentences to ensure that they understand their meanings. Students who easily master these sorts can also create additional contractions beyond those already included in the sorts using the verbs *is*, *are*, *will*, *have*, and *would*.

Standard Weekly Routines for Use with Sorts 46–49

Follow the series of instructional procedures outlined on pages 26–28 with these sorts, including learning and practicing the vocabulary, working repeatedly with the sorts, providing extension activities, and conducting informal assessments. A spell check is included in this unit as a post-assessment. As described earlier, this chapter invites investigations into how these words fit into the context of a complete sentence. Whenever opportunities arise, interchange the contracted words with the two words they stand for to check that students understand their meanings. Play guessing games or matching games that require students to take apart and rebuild the contractions multiple times. This mastery learning will help students to easily move back and forth between a contraction and the words it comes from. Use both oral and written informal assessments to ensure that students are gaining facility with producing and applying the words being studied. Use the results of your informal assessments to plan additional support as needed. Encourage word hunts to find additional contractions, and discuss these new words in your word study lessons. When you find a word with an apostrophe, analyze it to find out whether it is a contraction, is missing some letters, or is showing possession.

Literature Connection

Because contractions are plentiful in oral and written language, many children's literature books have examples to highlight. Select books from your classroom or school library, or seek out the following literature to explore contractions. When possible, use sentences in the books as frames to create new sentences using the contracted word. For example, "We're going on a ______ hunt" is a common theme in literature. Encourage your students to devise new sentences and stories using this familiar pattern. The following books highlight sentences with contractions that you and your students can enjoy and build upon.

Axtell, D. (1999). *We're going on a lion hunt.* New York: Henry Holt & Company.

Hoberman, M. (2003). *And to think that we thought we would never be friends.* Decorah, IA: Dragonfly Books.

Krasnesky, T. (2010). *That cat can't stay.* Chicago, IL: Independent Publishers Group/ Flashlight Press.

Leedy, L. (2003). *There's a frog in my throat! 440 animal sayings a little bird told me.* New York: Holiday House.

Lyons, S. (2009). *If you were an apostrophe.* Mankato, MN: Picture Window Books.

Metzger, S. (2005). *We're going on a leaf hunt.* New York: Scholastic.

Rabe, T. (1999). *There's no place like space!* New York: Random House.

Shaskan, T. S. (2008). *If you were a contraction.* Mankato, MN: Picture Window Books.

Sturges, P. (2004). *She'll be comin' 'round the mountain.* New York: Little Brown.

Truss, L. (2012). *The girl's like spaghetti.* New York: Scholastic Cartwheel.

Demonstrate, Sort, Check, and Reflect

(See pages 132–135.) Prepare a set of words to use for teacher-directed modeling for Sort 46: *Contraction Matching.*

1. Point out that this week's sort is a little different because it involves matching pairs of words with another word—called a *contraction*—that is another way of saying the same thing. When something is *contracted* it means it shrinks or grows smaller; a contraction is a shortened version of a word. Introduce the words and word pairs in the sort and discuss any that are unfamiliar or difficult. Learn and practice unknown vocabulary words as described in the standard weekly routines on pages 26–28. Ask students what they notice about the words or word pairs (they either have two words that together mean something, or they contain an apostrophe). Point out that all of the single words are contractions and contain the apostrophe mark that shows where some letters have been taken out. Say the

words aloud together, emphasizing the sounds in the contractions. Next, work your way through each of the words or word pairs, saying it aloud and deciding whether it belongs in the **we're** column (for contractions), or the **we are** column (for word pairs). Hold up one word card at a time and ask students to say the word or words and help you sort them into the appropriate column. *"Where does* he is *belong? Yes, it goes in the column with* we are *because it is two words and not a contraction."* Continue with the students' help until all the words have been sorted. Let mistakes go for now.

2. When all the words have been sorted, have the students join in as you name them from top to bottom in the columns and check for any that need to be changed. *"Do all of these cards have two words? Are the words in this column contractions? Do we need to move any?"* The next step in the sort is to match up the word pairs with their contraction partners. Work from one word pair to the next and have students help you find a match. *"Here is the word pair* they are. *Let's find the contraction that means the same thing and is spelled in almost the same way. Yes,* they're *means they are. Look at the apostrophe in the word* they're. *What letter or letters does the apostrophe stand for? Right, the* a *is missing."* Continue in this manner until you have matched all of the word pairs and contractions.

3. Repeat the sort with the group. This time, you may want to mix up the words, turn them face down in a deck, and let students take turns drawing a card and sorting it in the correct column (contraction/word pair). You can also simply pass out the cards and have the students take turns sorting them. After sorting, have students match the contractions and word pairs so they are side by side in the two columns. Have students read the word pairs along with the contraction partners so they hear the similarities and differences in pronunciation, and compare the written forms of each item.

4. Give each student a copy of the sort for individual practice. Assign the task of cutting out the word cards and then sorting on their own in the same way they did in the group. Ask students to sort their cards by contractions versus word pairs and then match up the items with the same meaning. On subsequent days students should repeat the sorting activity several times. Involve the students in the other standard weekly routines described in this text and in *WTW EL* for the within word pattern stage.

5. Informally assess students on the contractions under study throughout the week. Observe students' accuracy and fluency in sorting, their pronunciation of the words, and their knowledge of the English vocabulary. At the end of the week, call out some of the contractions you have been working with and ask students to think about what letters are missing and where the apostrophe needs to be placed when these words are written.

Extend

Provide numerous opportunities for students to read, write, and engage with the words in the sorts. An especially useful activity will be to engage with a sentence frame chart using some of the words in the sort. In a sentence frame activity, the teacher constructs a model sentence such as, "We are interested in playing soccer." Then, the underlined words are substituted with others as students create their own sentences (Dutro & Helman, 2009). A simple version of a sentence frame might be to ask students to exchange the word pair for the contraction that matches and add their own word at the end. A more complex version would be for students to insert other contractions that still make sense within the sentence context (e.g., *she's, he's, they're*). Add or take away possible word cards to challenge or provide extra support as needed. For students with advanced English language skills, sentences can become more complex, such as, "If she hadn't seen me, I never would've found my way home." (e.g., "If they weren't with me, I never would've had so much fun.").

Dutro, S., & Helman, L. (2009). Explicit language instruction: A key to constructing meaning. In L. Helman (Ed.), *Literacy Development with English Learners: Research-Based Instruction in Grades K-6* (pp. 40–63). New York: The Guilford Press.

Board games, card games, and picture dictionaries are especially fun ways to match contractions with their word pair partners. Create a classroom chart or a page in students' word study notebooks to add other contractions and the words they came from. How many letters are usually taken out to create a contraction? Are there oddballs that do not directly match their partners?

Completed sorts for this chapter should look something like the following tables. Notes that are specific to individual sorts are included above each table of sorted words.

Sort 46: Contraction Matching

(See page 132.)

we are	**we're**
they will	they'll
she would	she'd
did not	didn't
could have	could've
was not	wasn't
they are	they're
where is	where's
what is	what's
are not	aren't
he is	he's
there is	there's

***Additional words:** we will/we'll, we did/we'd, she will/she'll, he did/he'd, he will/he'll, they did/they'd, would have/would've, I will/I'll, I would/I'd*

Sort 47: Word Sort with *'s, 're,* and *'ll*

(See page 133.) In this sort students sort contractions that are based on words with *is* (*'s*), *are* (*'re*), and *will* (*'ll*).

's* for *is	***'re* for *are***	***'ll* for *will***
she's	what're	we'll
who's	they're	I'll

's for is	're for are	'll for will
he's	we're	they'll
where's	you're	you'll
it's		she'll
that's		who'll
there's		what'll
how's		
what's		
here's		

Additional words: *when's, why's, where're, when're, he'll, that'll, it'll*

Sort 48: Word Sort with *n't* and *'ve*

(See page 134.) In this sort students sort contractions that are based on words with *not* (*n't*) and *have* (*'ve*).

n't for not	've for have
didn't	we've
hadn't	I've
couldn't	could've
shouldn't	you've
isn't	they've
weren't	should've
can't	would've
haven't	you've
won't	might've
doesn't	
don't	
aren't	
wasn't	

Additional words: *hasn't, mustn't, wouldn't, might've, what've, who've*

Sort 49: Word Sort with *'d and 'll*

(See page 135.) In this sort students sort contractions that are based on words with *would* (*'d*) and *will* (*'ll*).

'd for *would*	*'ll* for *will*
I'd	they'll
who'd	we'll
what'd	she'll
you'd	how'll
where'd	what'll
she'd	you'll
he'd	where'll
how'd	who'll
they'd	this'll
this'd	he'll
we'd	I'll

Additional words: *there'd, it'll*

Spell Check: Contractions

(See page 136.) This assessment is presented in a writing sort format and checks for correct spelling of contractions with *'ve, 'll, n't, 're, 's,* and *'d*. All of the 18 words have been sorted in Sorts 46–49. Copy and enlarge page 136 for all students you wish to participate in the assessment. Say each word clearly and use it in a simple sentence. Ask students to write the word in the box labeled with the correct ending to the word. For example, if you call out the word *I'd* it would be written in the **would ('d)** box. If you are grading this spell check, give one point for writing the word in the correct category and another point for the correct spelling of the entire word.

Call out the words in the order presented below. Say each word once, use it in a sentence, and then say it again. Following are the 18 words assessed:

1. she'd **2.** he's **3.** can't
4. we've **5.** what'll **6.** isn't
7. you're **8.** I've **9.** he'd
10. don't **11.** I'll **12.** we're
13. you'd **14.** haven't **15.** who's
16. you've **17.** we'll **18.** they'd

SORTS 46–49

SORT 46: Contraction Matching

we are	**we're**	they will
he is	didn't	she would
what's	could've	did not
she'd	was not	there is
they are	he's	where's
could have	where is	are not
they'll	wasn't	they're
aren't	there's	what is

SORT 47: Word Sort with *'s, 're,* and *'ll*

's for *is*	**'re for *are***	**'ll for *will***
you're	who's	I'll
he's	we'll	what're
she'll	where's	she's
they're	it's	we're
who'll	they'll	how's
there's	here's	that's
you'll	what's	what'll

SORT 48: Word Sort with *n't* and *'ve*

n't* for *not	***'ve* for *have***	didn't
I've	couldn't	we've
can't	would've	hadn't
haven't	shouldn't	won't
could've	isn't	they've
doesn't	weren't	should've
you've	might've	don't
aren't	wasn't	you've

SORT 49: Word Sort with *'d* and *'ll*

***'d* for would**	***'ll* for *will***	I'd
she'd	you'll	they'll
what'll	where'd	we'll
how'd	he'd	who'd
where'll	this'll	what'd
this'd	they'd	she'll
who'll	I'll	you'd
he'll	we'd	how'll

SPELL CHECK: *Contractions*

1. *have ('ve)*	2. *will ('ll)*	3. *not (n't)*
4. *are ('re)*	**5. *is ('s)***	**6. *would ('d)***

unit

11

Homophones

Notes for the Teacher

Homophones are words that sound the same but have different meanings, such as the words *plane* and *plain.* Throughout their study of the vowel patterns in this text students have seen and discussed many homophones, and Unit 6 explicitly introduced the concept of a homophone. Because homophones present many opportunities to do vocabulary study and investigate spelling patterns, this text includes two units on the topic. The current unit circles around to the learning students did previously on homophones, this time including words with more complex spelling patterns. Introducing so many spelling patterns to students earlier, prior to their being proficient as within word pattern spellers, would have likely been quite frustrating. It is hoped that now that students have a solid knowledge of many vowel patterns in single-syllable words, this unit will be challenging but not overwhelming. As in the previous homophone unit, there are multiple opportunities to explore the meanings of words and reinforce their spelling patterns here, and we invite you to engage in many activities that will help students understand homophones better.

There are four sorts and a spell check in this unit. The first three sorts examine homophones based on the long-vowel sound they employ. For example, Sort 50: *Homophones with ā* features word pairs such as *male/mail, bear/bare,* and *eight/ate.* Sorts 51 and 52 feature words with the ō and ē sounds. Sort 53 explores other spelling patterns that may form homophones, such as those in the words *I/eye, fir/fur,* and *its/it's.* As students work with these sets of homophones, they continue to expand their understanding of the many ways a word may be spelled and how the pattern used signifies the word's meaning. Once students make the spelling-meaning connection for a particular homophone, they can use this understanding to spell other related words correctly as well. For example, once a student clearly understands the difference between *sale* and *sail,* other words and phrases should become easier to spell, such as *sailboat, for sale,* or *yard sale.*

After completing these sorts, your students will have a deeper understanding of common homophones and should develop the habit of asking themselves what a word means before they try to spell it. The more opportunities they have to read, discuss, and work with the words in these sorts, the more likely they are to retain their spelling patterns and apply them in their own writing.

Standard Weekly Routines for Use with Sorts 50–53

1. **Learning and Practicing Unknown Vocabulary** As in all of the previous sorts, it is important that your students know the meaning of each word in a sort. Preview the sort cards with your students to ensure they know what each item is. To clarify word meanings,

you might ask students to draw a picture on the back of the word card. For example, on the back of the *break* card, a student might draw a broken pencil. On the back of the *brake* card, a student might draw a car because it has brakes to help it stop. Take the time to discuss all of the words and compare the meanings of the homophone pairs. It may be wise to start with half of the sorting words on the first day and add additional pairs each day. This will allow you to practice the vocabulary within the word study lesson. Talk about the words with students, clarify their meanings, and invite students to use them in sentences that connect to their lives. If possible, have students share with each other in Spanish to clarify the meaning of any unknown items.

2. **Repeated Work with the Words** Students should work with the featured sort several times after it has been modeled and discussed in a group. After cutting out the words and using them for individual practice, students can store the pieces in envelopes or baggies to sort again several times on other days. The pictures and words can also be used in partner activities during which students work together to read and spell the words. At some point students may glue the sort onto paper or use it to combine with additional sorts in review lessons.

3. **Writing** Invite students to create sentences that show they know the meanings of the homophone pairs and are using the appropriate spelling pattern, such as "The maid made the bed." Consider creating (or adding to) group books or personal homophone dictionaries that teach the spellings and meanings of a variety of homophones. Be sure to check in with students each time they are comparing homophone pairs to make sure they understand what each word refers to.

4. **Spelling** As you work with the sorts over the course of a week, have students quiz each other on the sounds, spellings, and meanings of the homophone pairs. Have them help each other think of ways to remember which word means what. Have students use their homophone dictionaries as a check.

5. **Games and Other Activities** Create matching games or silly stories or build words with letter tiles to reinforce how the spelling of a homophone determines its meaning. Encourage students to notice homophones they encounter in their reading materials and add them to class bulletin boards or vocabulary word walls.

6. **Assessment** To assess students' weekly mastery, ask them to spell and read the words. Because there is a limited number of homophones in this unit, you can administer a traditional spelling test using the words, or you can dictate some of the featured words of the week. Have students number their papers or white boards and call aloud a sample of words from the lesson. Discuss any words that are mixed up with the incorrect homophone partner. A spell check is included at the end of this unit and is intended to serve as a post-assessment.

Literature Connection

The following books feature homophones in interesting ways. Use these books or others that you know of as jumping off points to reinforce the concept of homophones. The pictures will help students learn new vocabulary and make the learning fun. These books are great models to use in creating student-made books in the classroom, too.

Cleary, B. P., & Gable, B. (2005). *How much can a bare bear bear?* Fresno, CA: Millbrook Press.

Gwynne, F. (1988). *The king who rained.* New York: Aladdin Paperbacks.

Scheunemann, P. (2002). *The moose is in the mousse.* Minneapolis, MN: ABDO Publishing Co. (See also others in the homophone series.)

Demonstrate, Sort, Check, and Reflect

(See pages 143–146.) Prepare a set of words to use for teacher-directed modeling, such as for Sort 50: *Homophones with* ā.

1. Introduce the words in the sort and discuss any that are unfamiliar. Learn and practice unknown vocabulary words as described in the standard weekly routines on pages 137–138. Ask students to help you match the homophone partners so that you can compare their meanings and spellings. What do they notice about the words? (They sound the same but they have different spellings and meanings.) Point out that the words are spelled with a variety of spelling patterns, but they all have the sound of the long *a*. Put up the header cards for **mail** and **male**. Discuss the meanings and spellings of these words. "Mail *that is spelled m-a-i-l means a letter or package that gets sent to you.* Male *that is spelled m-a-l-e is a boy or man.*" Hold up one word card at a time and ask students to help you match it with its partner homophone. Always discuss the meaning of the words as you match them. For example, hold up the words *praise* and *prays* and ask, "*Who can share what they know about these two words? How might we remember which one is something that means someone has something good to say about you, and the other is something people might do in church?*" Continue with the students' help until all the words have been matched.
2. When all the words have been matched, have the students review the spelling patterns with you across each pair, and place the words in different columns according to the vowel pattern used. The headers should include: **ai, a_e, ay, ea, ei,** and **ey**. "*Let's look at the words* mail *and* male. *Which column do each of these words belong in?*" Keep partner words on the same line regardless of what spelling pattern column they are put into.
3. Repeat the match and sort activity with the group. You may want to have students discuss the meaning of each word they match before they sort it into the correct spelling pattern column. You can also pass out the cards and have the students find any matches they have in their collection. Next, they can work with others in their group to pair up all of the words. Periodically check to see whether they remember the meaning of the word they are sorting. After sorting, model how to check by naming the words in each column and talking about how the words in each column are alike. This is a good opportunity to informally assess how easily your students can distinguish the extensive range of vowel patterns.
4. Give each student a copy of the sort for individual practice. Assign the task of cutting out the words and then matching and sorting on their own in the same way they did in the group. On subsequent days students should repeat the sorting activity several times. Involve the students in the other standard weekly routines described in this text and in *WTW EL* for the within word pattern stage.
5. Informally assess students on the vowel patterns and word meanings under study throughout the week. Observe students' accuracy and fluency in sorting and their knowledge of the English vocabulary. At the end of the week, call out some of the words you have been working with and ask students to think about which vowel pattern is used to create the long *a* sound in the word.

Extend

Provide numerous opportunities for students to read, write, and engage with the words in the sorts. Card games and silly stories are especially fun ways to review the words and talk about their spelling patterns. You may do a modeled writing activity for students in which you "accidentally" misspell a word (such as using *cheep* for *cheap*), then discuss out loud your thinking and change the spelling. This think-aloud process will provide an example for your students as they do their own writing.

Completed sorts 50–53 should look something like in the following tables.

Sort 50: Homophones with ā

(See page 143.)

ai	a_e	ay	ea	ei	ey
mail	**male**				
maid	made				
sail	sale				
plain	plane				
vain	vane				
	bare		bear		
	brake		break		
	stake		steak		
	ate		eight		
praise		prays			
wait				weight	
		pray			prey

***Additional words:** bass/base, fair/fare, flair/flare, grate/great, hair/hare, hay/hey, main/mane, pail/pale, pear/pare/pair, rain/rein/reign, rays/raze/raise, wail/whale*

Sort 51: Homophones with ō

(See page 144.) This sort examines common homophone pairs that feature a long *o* sound. Follow the procedures listed in Demonstrate, Sort, Check, and Reflect and Extend outlined on page 139, but set up columns as with **oa, o_e, ou/ow, oll, or,** and **_o.** As you demonstrate the sort, discuss the various ways to create the long *o* sound in words.

oa	o_e	ou/ow	oll	or	_o
road	**rode**				
boar	bore				
loan	lone				
board	bored				

oa	o_e	ou/ow	oll	or	_o
	role		roll		
	pole		poll		
	rose	rows			
	close, clothes				
		four		for	
		know			no
		pour		poor	
groan		grown			

***Additional words:** hoarse/horse, ore/or/oar, ode/owed, sole/soul, throne/thrown, toad/towed*

Sort 52: Homophones with ē

(See page 145.) This sort examines common homophone pairs that feature a long *e* sound. Follow the procedures listed in Demonstrate, Sort, Check, and Reflect and Extend outlined on page 139, but set up columns as with **ea, ee, e_e,** and **_e**. As you demonstrate the sort, discuss the various ways to create the long *e* sound in words.

ee	ea	e_e	_e
deer	**dear**		
heel	heal		
meet	meat		
tee	tea		
cheep	cheap		
creek	creak		
see	sea		
wee			we
bee			be
seen		scene	
	jeans	genes	
	hear	here	

***Additional words:** flee/flea, knead/need, peek/peak, read/reed, real/reel, steal/steel, weak/week*

Sort 53: Other Homophones

(See page 146.) This sort examines other homophone pairs that have not been studied in this unit. Follow the procedures listed in Demonstrate, Sort, Check, and Reflect and Extend outlined on page 139 to match the homophone pairs, but do not worry about sorting the pairs by their spelling patterns. Instead, use the sort as material for examining the many ways punctuation marks and vowels and consonants can be used to create the same sounds in different words.

I	**eye**
our	hour
witch	which
or	oar
fined	find
we'd	weed
fur	fir
hay	hey
high	hi
its	it's
horse	hoarse
not	knot

Additional words: *ad/add, by/buy/bye, cell/sell, cent/scent/sent, chews/choose, die/dye, do/due/dew, find/fined, flew/flu, knew/new, shoe/shoo, son/sun, theirs/there's, whose/who's*

Spell Check: Assessment for Homophones

(See page 147.) This assessment is presented in a cloze format. Students must recall the correct spelling of the homophone that will complete each sentence and write it in the blank provided. Students can do this spell check silently on their own, or you can read the sentences aloud as they view the page. The sentences, and their answers, are as follows:

1. I fell when my shoe lost its *heel.*
2. I put the letter in the *mail.*
3. The number after seven is *eight.*
4. She can jump off a diving *board.*
5. The store is having a big *sale.*
6. Do you have money to give me a *loan*?
7. He will be here in the next *hour.*
8. Can you tie a *knot?*
9. The bird went way up *high.*
10. Do you like to drink *tea?*

SORTS 50–53

SORT 50: Homophones with $\bar{a}$

mail	**male**	bear
ate	sail	stake
weight	plane	pray
praise	maid	wait
sale	bare	vain
plain	break	prey
brake	eight	made
steak	prays	vane

SORT 51: Homophones with ō

road	**rode**	pole
for	clothes	loan
role	rows	bore
groan	poll	poor
boar	bored	rose
no	close	know
lone	board	pour
grown	four	roll

SORT 52: Homophones with $\bar{e}$

deer	**dear**	cheep
heel	we	jeans
be	here	bee
meet	heal	hear
tee	scene	creek
wee	cheap	seen
creak	see	meat
sea	genes	tea

SORT 53: Other Homophones

I	**eye**	fir
hay	hour	not
its	which	hi
or	hoarse	weed
fined	oar	find
we'd	our	it's
fur	knot	horse
high	hey	witch

SPELL CHECK: Assessment for Homophones

1. I fell when my shoe lost its ______________________.

heel heal

2. I put the letter in the ______________________.

male mail

3. The number after seven is ______________________.

ate eight

4. She can jump off a diving ______________________.

bored board

5. The store is having a big ______________________.

sail sale

6. Do you have money to give me a ______________________?

lone loan

7. He will be here in the next ______________________.

hour our

8. Can you tie a ______________________?

knot not

9. The bird went way up ______________________.

hi high

10. Do you like to drink ______________________?

tee tea

unit

12

Introduction to Two-Syllable, High-Frequency Words

Notes for the Teacher

In this unit we enter the world of two-syllable words. Up until now in this text, all of the sorts have focused on single-syllable words for students to work on understanding and using the long-vowel and other patterns found in English. In Sorts 54 and 55, students engage with high-frequency words that they have likely seen frequently in their reading materials and used regularly in their written work. These words have one unaccented syllable that makes them tricky to spell, so students will need to rely on their knowledge of how to spell the vowel pattern in the accented syllable and use other support strategies to remember the unaccented component. This introductory unit begins the transition from within word pattern word study to that of syllables and affixes, where the focus turns to multi-syllable words.

There are two sorts and a spell check in this unit. The first sort examines high-frequency words starting with *a-* and *be-* such as *alive* and *below*. Other commonly used high-frequency words such as *enough* and *money* are also included for students to engage with as well. In Sort 55 students investigate high-frequency words ending with *–le* and *–y*. These common words serve as an initial opportunity to investigate, reflect upon, and discuss longer words that students have seen many times. As students work with the words in these two sorts, they are called on to apply the vowel patterns they have been studying within a controlled context. If you find that students have difficulty representing the short-vowel, long-vowel, or other vowel patterns represented in the stressed part of the word, review these patterns before moving ahead. For example, if students are unable to spell the *cross* in *across*, or the *fore* in *before*, take a step back to discuss and practice how short-vowel, long-vowel, and other vowel patterns are constructed.

After completing these sorts your students will have a deeper understanding of how they might tackle the spelling of a multi-syllable word by finding the syllable that can be best heard and represented by a particular vowel pattern. They will also see that some amount of study and concentration on the spelling of the other part of the word (unaccented) will be needed to cement its spelling in their minds. For this reason, the more opportunities students have to read, describe, and work with the words in these sorts, the more likely they are to retain their spelling patterns and apply them in their own writing.

Standard Weekly Routines for Use with Sorts 54–55

1. **Learning and Practicing Unknown Vocabulary** As in all of the previous sorts, it is important that your students know the meaning of each word in a sort. Because these words are highly frequent in oral and written language, knowing what they mean will likely not be a big problem. Still, it is important to preview the sort cards with your students to ensure they can use each item.
2. **Repeated Work with the Words** Students should work with the featured sort several times after it has been modeled and discussed in a group. After cutting out the words and using them for individual practice, students can store the pieces in envelopes or baggies to sort again several times on other days. The pictures and words can also be used in partner activities where students work together to read and spell the words. At some point students may glue the sort onto paper or use it to combine with additional sorts in review lessons. If students find other high-frequency, two-syllable words they would like to add to their sorting cards, that is fine, too.
3. **Writing** Students are likely to have used the words in this unit quite frequently in their writing. It is also likely that they have frequently misspelled them. Ask students to look through their personal writing to find any of the sorting words, highlight them, and see whether they are spelled correctly. If words are misspelled, have students make notes about what would help them remember the "tricky part." Share these reflections in word study group activities.
4. **Spelling** As you work with the sort over the course of a week, have students quiz each other on the sounds and patterns of the high-frequency words. Have them help each other think of ways to remember how each word is spelled. Consider using a routine that allows them to (a) identify trouble spots as well as familiar chunks in a word, (b) self-correct a pre-test, (c) work through the self-study method that includes look-say-write-check, and (d) participate in spell checks.
5. **Games and Other Activities** Games provide an opportunity to build familiarity with the correct spelling of the words, to have discussions about the features of words, and to practice memory techniques. Especially useful games for this unit's words might be Concentration/Memory, Go Fish, or the Racetrack board game from *WTW EL*.
6. **Assessment** To assess students' weekly mastery, ask them to spell and read the words. You can administer a traditional spelling test using the words, or you can use white boards to dictate a selection of the words of the week. Have students number their papers or white boards and call aloud a sample of words from the lesson. Because the words are very common, it will also be important to hold students accountable for correctly spelling these words in their independent writing. A spell check is included at the end of this unit and is intended to serve as a post-assessment.

Literature Connection

The following books include those that feature two-syllable, high-frequency words as well as a few books that focus on an interest in words. As you read them with your students, notice any of the sorting words of the week and review their spelling patterns. Use these books to help instill a curiosity for words and how they are written.

Balouch, K. (2006). *Mystery bottle*. New York: Hyperion Books.

Degross, M. (1998). *Donovan's word jar*. New York: HarperTrophy.

Heller, R. (1993). *Animals born alive and well*. New York: Penguin Putnam Books for Young Readers.

Mora, P. (2000). *Tomás and the library lady*. Decorah, IA: Dragonfly Books.

Prelutsky, J. (2005). *It's raining pigs and noodles*. New York: Greenwillow Books.

Schotter, R. (2006). *The boy who loved words*. New York: Schwartz & Wade.

Shapiro, K. J. (2007). *I must go down to the beach again*. Watertown, MA: Charlesbridge Publishing.

Stone, R. (1975). *Because a little bug went ka-choo!* New York: Random House.

Wadsworth, G. (2009). *Up, up, and away*. Watertown, MA: Charlesbridge Publishing.

Demonstrate, Sort, Check, and Reflect

(See pages 154–155.) Prepare a set of words to use for teacher-directed modeling, such as for Sort 54: *High-Frequency Words Starting with* a- *and* be-.

1. Tell students that beginning this week you will be working with longer words, words with more than one syllable. They will begin with words that should be familiar to them from their reading and writing. Introduce the words in the sort and discuss any that are unfamiliar. Point out the three column headers for the sort: ***a- alive, be- below,*** and ***other***. As you read each word with the group, help students to "pull off" the *a-*, *be-*, or other first syllable. Sort the words into one of the three groups.
2. When all the words have been sorted, discuss the variety of vowel spelling patterns they contain. Point out that by pulling the syllables apart it often becomes easier to spell at least half of the word. Compare the long-vowel, short-vowel, and other vowel spellings that are apparent in each word.
3. Repeat the sort activity with the group, this time discussing the vowel pattern in the strong syllable. You may want to have students think of single-syllable words they know that have the same vowel sound and pattern. You can also pass out the cards and have the students sort the words in their collection. After sorting, model how to check by naming the words in each column and then talk about how the words in each column are alike. This is a good opportunity to informally assess how easily your students can distinguish the extensive range of vowel patterns.
4. Give each student a copy of the sort for individual practice. Assign the task of cutting out the words and then matching and sorting on their own in the same way they did in the group. On subsequent days students should repeat the sorting activity several times. Involve the students in the other standard weekly routines described in this text and in *WTW EL* for the late within word pattern stage.
5. Informally assess students on the words under study throughout the week. Observe students' accuracy and fluency in sorting and their ability to use the words correctly in their writing. At the end of the week, call out some of the words you have been working with and ask students to think about how they would pull the word apart to make it easier to spell.

Extend

Provide numerous opportunities for students to read, write, and engage with the words in the sorts. Go on a word hunt or review classroom word walls for two-syllable, high-frequency words to add to the sorts in this chapter. Add these words to storytelling or writing activities in class to get more exposure and repetition with them.

Completed Sorts 54 and 55 should look something like in the following tables.

Sort 54: High-Frequency Words Starting with *a-* and *be-*

(See page 154.)

a- alive	be- below	other
ago	began	money
away	between	enough
asleep	begin	over
above	before	until
across	because	upon
ahead	believe	
again		
about		
around		
along		

Additional words: *afraid, agreed, alone, amount, became, become, behind, belong, beside, water, mother, under, second*

Sort 55: High-Frequency Words Ending with *-le* and *-y*

(See page 155.) This sort examines another set of high-frequency words, this time with unstressed ending syllables. As in Sort 54, encourage students to break the words in two and become familiar with how the vowels and endings are spelled.

-y any	-le little
tiny	people
hurry	couple
body	eagle
city	castle
only	simple
story	apple
baby	bottle
pretty	double
country	circle
very	
party	
pony	
many	

***Additional words:** study, carry, really, easy, middle, uncle, battle, cattle, pickle*

Spell Check: Assessment for High-Frequency, Two-Syllable Words

(See page 156.) This assessment is presented in a writing sort format. All of the words assessed have been studied in this unit. Photocopy and enlarge page 156 for all students you wish to participate in the post-test. Say each word clearly and ask your students to write the word in the box with the correct beginning or ending syllable. For example, if you call out the word *above*, it should be written in the *a-* column. If you call out the word *little*, it should be written in the *-le* column.

Call out the words in the following order and use each word in a sentence to make sure your students understand what word you are saying. Say each word once, use it in a sentence, then say it again.

1. alive	**2.** pretty	**3.** began
4. ahead	**5.** circle	**6.** ago
7. because	**8.** little	**9.** story
10. simple	**11.** many	**12.** party
13. very	**14.** between	**15.** people
16. city	**17.** only	**18.** around

Allow time for the students to check and rewrite their words as needed. The answer sheet will look like this:

a-	be-	-y	-le
alive	began	pretty	circle
ahead	because	story	little
ago	between	many	simple
around		party	people
		very	
		city	
		only	

SORTS 54–55

SORT 54: High-Frequency Words Starting with *a-* and *be-*

a- alive	**be- below**	**other**
across	because	ago
began	over	before
again	around	until
about	enough	believe
between	ahead	away
along	money	upon
begin	above	asleep

SORT 55: High-Frequency Words Ending with *-le* and *-y*

-y any	**-le little**	tiny
pretty	story	people
simple	baby	hurry
very	circle	couple
apple	country	body
pony	double	eagle
many	party	city
bottle	only	castle

SPELL CHECK: Assessment for High-Frequency, Two-Syllable Words

1. a-	2. be-	3. -y	4. -le

unit

13

Introduction to Inflectional Endings with Plural and Past Tense

Notes for the Teacher

In the final unit of this text we guide students to acquire a conceptual understanding of the plural endings *-s* and *-es* and of the past tense *–ed*. This series of sorts is designed for students at the late within word pattern stage. Although it isn't until the next stage, syllables and affixes, that students begin to examine how the base word changes to accommodate word endings, it is important that students first understand plural and past tense endings as purposeful units that carry meaning within a word. When writers or speakers in English want to indicate more than one object, they often add an *–s* or *–es*. When writers or speakers want to show that something already happened, they often do that by adding *–ed*. Students in the late within word pattern stage may still spell these inflectional endings phonetically, as in GLASSIS or HELPT.

English learners may vary in their mastery of these grammatical forms in their speech. Some students may accurately use and pronounce the three sounds of *–ed* (e.g., ***mailed***, ***added***, ***jumped***) and say plural words with the appropriate number of syllables (e.g., *beaches* vs. *friends*). Other students may be learning correct pronunciation of plurals and past tense words at the same time as they learn to write them accurately. Because late within word pattern spellers are reading and writing many words with these common inflectional endings, it is a good time for students to learn the conventional spelling of plurals and past tense. By addressing the grammatical function and meaning along with the spelling pattern, it is hoped that English learners will gain insights into both *what* the endings mean, along with *how* they are written. Changes to the base word to accommodate these endings, such as consonant doubling, dropping the final *e*, or changing *y* to *i*, will not be addressed here. These more complicated conventions are addressed in the syllables and affixes stage.

Studying inflectional endings provides a great opportunity for exploring many grammatical features of English such as subject and verb agreement, verb tense, and how word parts convey meaning as well as sound. In Spanish, plurals are constructed in a similar manner to English. For example, sometimes *–s* is added to a word to create a plural (e.g., *casa-casas*), and other times *–es* is added (e.g., *mujer-mujeres*). This commonality can be pointed out to Spanish-speaking students. Creating a past tense verb, however, is quite different and more complex in Spanish. This may be one of the few occasions when students find that English has a grammatical process that is a bit simpler!

As students work through the sorts, identify plurals and past tense words in their reading texts, and use sentence frames to practice them in their writing activities, many opportunities will surface for you to clarify and correct confusions. Informal assessments and this unit's spell check will guide you to identify students who need additional explanation, practice, or other support. If you notice that students are not using the inflectional endings correctly, slow your instruction, listen to how students pronounce and use the words, and provide more explicit direction.

Sort 56 in this unit helps students to see that plurals mean "more than one." In the sort, students work with common words that have both *-s* and *-es* endings. Sort 57 asks students to notice which words use *-s* and which use *-es* to create the plural. After this initial sort, students examine how the base word ending influences the use of *-s* or *-es*. Sort 58 helps students understand that the ending *-ed* is frequently used to mean something that happened in the past. Next, Sort 59 investigates the three sounds that *-ed* makes in a range of common words. Throughout this unit, students are encouraged to use the inflectional endings they are studying in the context of full sentences with both the focus words and other classroom-embedded examples.

Standard Weekly Routines for Use with Sorts 56–59

Follow the series of instructional procedures outlined on pages 26–28 with these sorts, including learning and practicing the vocabulary, working repeatedly with the sorts, providing extension activities, and conducting informal assessments. A spell check is included in this unit as a post-assessment. As described previously, this unit invites investigations into how these words fit into the context of a complete sentence. Consider playing oral language games prior to working with the sort words, such as converting singular nouns into plural nouns (e.g., *tree-trees, sandwich-sandwiches*) or changing a present tense verb to the past tense (e.g., *rain-rained*). Don't worry if some irregular words come up as you play these games—not all words become plurals by adding *-s* or *-es*, or change to the past tense with *-ed*. Just ask students to pay keen attention to the words that do follow the pattern.

Literature Connection

Plural and past tense words are common in children's literature, so you won't need to look further than your classroom bookshelf to find plenty of examples. The books in the following list provide numerous illustrations of inflectional endings in action and are a good starting place for your explorations and discussions.

Collandro, L. (2012). *There was an old lady who swallowed a book.* New York: Scholastic Cartwheel.

Henkes, K. (1986). *A weekend with Wendell.* New York: Greenwillow Books.

James, S. (1997). *Leon and Bob.* Somerville, MA: Candlewick Press.

Jeffers, O. (2007). *The incredible book-eating boy.* New York: Philomel.

Markle, S. (2009). *Foxes (animal predators).* Minneapolis, MN: Lerner Books.

Mathews, L. (1990). *Bunches and bunches of bunnies.* New York: Scholastic.

Scieszka, J. (1994). *The book that Jack wrote.* New York: Puffin.

Seuss, D. (1990). *Oh, the places you'll go!* New York: Random House.

Shaskan, T. S. (2009). *If you were a plural word.* Mankato, MN: Picture Window Books.

Demonstrate, Sort, Check, and Reflect

(See pages 164–167.) Prepare a set of words to use for teacher-directed modeling for Sort 56: *Singular and Plural Nouns.*

1. Introduce the words in the sort and discuss any that are unfamiliar or difficult. Learn and practice unknown vocabulary words as described in the standard weekly routines on pages 26–28. Point out that all of the words in this sort represent objects, even though some of them might have another meaning. For example, the word *watch* could mean "look at," but in this sort it means a clock that you typically wear on your wrist. Ask students what they notice about the words (there are pairs; some have *s* at the end and others don't). Begin reading the words, emphasizing the ending sound. Work through each of the words, saying each aloud and deciding whether it belongs in the **one** column (singular objects) or the **more than one** column (plurals). Hold up one word card at a time and ask students to say the word and help you sort it into the column where it belongs. *"Where does* snakes *belong? Yes, it goes in the column with* more than one *because it means more than one snake."* Continue with the students' help until all the words have been sorted. Let mistakes go for now.
2. When all the words have been sorted, have the students join in as you name them from top to bottom in the columns and check for any that need to be changed. *"Do all of these words stand for a single thing? Do the words in this column stand for more than one? Do we need to move any?"* Next, have students match the singular and plural of the same word and compare how they are written. *"What is the difference between how* snake *and* snakes *are written? What about* watch *and* watches*?"*
3. Repeat the sort with the group. This time you may want to mix up the words, turn them face down in a deck this time, and let students take turns drawing a card and sorting it in the correct column (**one/more than one**). You can also simply pass out the cards and have the students take turns sorting them. After sorting, have students match the singular and plural words so they are side by side in the two columns. Have students read the word pairs so they hear the differences in pronunciation, and compare the written forms of each item.
4. Give each student a copy of the sort for individual practice. Assign the task of cutting out the word cards and then sorting on their own in the same way they did in the group. Ask students to sort their cards by one versus more than one, and then match the words with the same base. On subsequent days students should repeat the sorting activity several times. Involve the students in the other standard weekly routines described in this text and in *WTW EL* for the within word pattern stage.
5. Informally assess students on the plurals under study throughout the week. Observe students' accuracy and fluency in sorting, their pronunciation of the words, and their knowledge of the English vocabulary. At the end of the week, call out some of the plurals you have been working with and ask students to think about the differences in spelling for words that indicate "more than one."

Extend

Provide numerous opportunities for students to read, write, and transform words using inflectional endings. An especially useful activity will be to engage with a sentence frame chart in which students alter sentences as needed to accommodate a changed word. For example, using a sentence frame, the teacher constructs a model sentence such as, "I saw a house on my way home." Then, the underlined words are substituted with others as students create their own sentences (e.g., three houses; Dutro & Helman, 2009). For past tense endings, students might transform the sentence from the present to the past as in,

"I walk to the store." This sentence could be transformed to "I walked to the store" or "She walked to the store." For students with advanced English language skills, sentences can become more complex, such as, "I usually walk to the store, but yesterday I skipped instead."

You can create small word cards for each of the inflectional endings *-s*, *-es*, and *-ed*. Ask students what types of words they could attach each ending to and let them try out making new words by adding endings. This activity is good practice for the taking-apart activities they will do in greater depth in the syllables and affixes stage that is coming next.

Completed sorts for this unit should look something like the following tables. Notes that are specific to individual sorts are included above each table of sorted words.

Sort 56: Singular and Plural Nouns

(See page 164.)

one	more than one
cup	cups
snake	snakes
fox	foxes
book	books
table	tables
watch	watches
nose	noses
nut	nuts
house	houses
class	classes
desk	desks

Additional words: *bird/birds, chin/chins, church/churches, dime/dimes, box/boxes, globe/globes, switch/switches, lamb/lambs*

Sort 57: Word Sort for Plural Endings

(See page 165.) In this sort students categorize words that need *-s* or *-es* to form a plural.

Dutro, S., & Helman, L. (2009). Explicit language instruction: A key to constructing meaning. In L. Helman (Ed.) *Literacy Development with English Learners: Research-Based Instruction in Grades K-6* (pp. 40–63). New York: The Guilford Press.

+s pigs	+es foxes
friends	inches
chairs	speeches
eyes	brushes
horses	splashes
boats	boxes
pants	beaches
beds	dresses
dogs	dishes
tests	glasses
miles	churches
cows	lunches

***Additional words:** wishes, benches, peaches, riches, taxes, keys, girls, trees, papers, cups, streets*

Sort 58: Present and Past Tense Verbs

(See page 166.) In this sort students categorize verbs that are in the present tense or use *-ed* to form the past tense.

present *mail*	past *mailed*
turn	turned
mix	mixed
walk	walked
clean	cleaned
need	needed
look	looked
help	helped
play	played
jump	jumped
burn	burned
show	showed

***Additional words:** bang/banged, cheer/cheered, blink/blinked, brush/brushed, burn/burned, float/floated, lift/lifted, pack/packed*

Sort 59: Word Sort for Past Tense Endings

(See page 167.) In this sort students categorize past tense verbs by the sound that the *-ed* represents in each word: /d/, /id/, or /t/.

/d/ mailed	**/id/ added**	**/t/ helped**
played	heated	crashed
leaned	needed	looked
feared	faded	marked
snowed	started	mixed
burned	lifted	knocked
showed	landed	reached
	flooded	passed
		coached

***Additional words:** rained, sailed, rolled, combed, dusted, hunted, landed, pointed, kissed, pushed, winked, brushed*

Spell Check: Inflectional Endings with Plural and Past Tense

(See page 168.) This assessment is presented in a simple dictation format. All 12 of the words have been sorted in Sorts 56–59. Copy and enlarge page 168 for all students you wish to participate in the assessment. Ask students to write the word on the line labeled with the number you call out. Remind them to think carefully about which type of ending is needed for the word they are spelling: *-s*, *-es*, or *-ed.* Call out the words in the order presented below using the sentences provided. Say each word once, give the sentence, and then say the word again. Following are the 12 words assessed as well as the model sentences:

1. *books* — We have many *books* in our classroom. — *books*
2. *foxes* — *Foxes* have bushy tails. — *foxes*
3. *miles* — How many *miles* do we have to drive? — *miles*
4. *helped* — She *helped* me find my bike. — *helped*
5. *lifted* — I *lifted* the box into the car. — *lifted*
6. *boats* — There were too many *boats* to count. — *boats*

7. *mailed*	They *mailed* the package to Grandma.	*mailed*
8. *needed*	I *needed* to find my sister.	*needed*
9. *dishes*	Will you help me do the *dishes*?	*dishes*
10. *inches*	The worm is five *inches* long.	*inches*
11. *mixed*	He *mixed* the juice with water.	*mixed*
12. *jumped*	The horse *jumped* over the fence.	*jumped*

SORTS 56–59

SORT 56: *Singular and Plural Nouns*

one	**more than one**	cup
snakes	watches	desk
nose	book	fox
watch	nuts	classes
nut	houses	snake
cups	table	foxes
noses	desks	tables
class	house	books

SORT 57: Word Sort for Plural Endings

+s pigs	**+es foxes**	pants
beaches	friends	inches
dogs	dishes	boats
tests	glasses	speeches
dresses	horses	beds
cows	lunches	splashes
churches	chairs	miles
boxes	eyes	brushes

SORT 58: Present and Past Tense Verbs

present *mail*	**past *mailed***	turn
mix	helped	clean
needed	walk	mixed
jump	cleaned	look
burn	turned	play
looked	need	showed
show	jumped	burned
played	help	walked

SORT 59: Word Sort for Past Tense Endings

/d/ mailed	***/id/ added***	***/t/ helped***
needed	looked	heated
faded	leaned	knocked
marked	passed	played
showed	flooded	crashed
mixed	landed	started
burned	coached	feared
reached	snowed	lifted

SPELL CHECK: Inflectional Endings with Plural and Past Tense

1.
2.
3.
4.
5.
6.
7.
8.
9.
10.
11.
12.

APPENDIX

Building, Blending, and Extending Cards

b	c	d	f	h
l	m	n	p	r
s	t	ch	sh	th
ph	cl	fl	sl	bl
gr	pr	br	cr	st

am	ame	at	ate
ope	ope	in	ine
id	ide	ut	ute

Blank Template for Word Sorts

Independent Word Study Directions

Name ______________________ Date ______________

1. Cut apart your words and sort them as you did in class. Pick a key word for each group, then write your words below the correct word.

____

____

____

____

____

____

____

____

____

____

2. What did you learn about words from this sort?

____

____

____

3. On the back of this paper write the same key words you used above. Ask someone to mix your word cards and read them to you one at a time as you write them into groups. Look at each word right after you write it. Correct it if you need to.

....

Check off what you did and ask a family member to sign below.

______ Sort the words again into the same groups as you did at school.

______ Write the words in groups as you copy them from the cards (#1).

______ Write about what you learned about words in this sort (#2).

______ Write the words into groups as someone reads them aloud (#3).

______ Find more words in your reading that have the same sound or pattern. Add them to the groups on the back.

Signature of family member ______________________________

Direcciones para el estudio de las palabras en casa

Nombre ______________________________ **Fecha** ______________

1. Corta tus palabras como lo hiciste en clase. Escoge una palabra clave para cada grupo, y luego escribe tus palabras debajo de la palabra clave correcta.

2. ¿Qué aprendiste sobre las palabras cuando hiciste esta clasificación?

3. Atrás de este papel escribe las mismas palabras claves que usaste arriba. Pide que alguien baraje las tarjetas de palabras y leértelas una a la vez mientras las escribes en los grupos. Mira bien a cada palabra después de escribirla. Corrígela si no está bien escrita.

Haz una X en cada tarea que terminaste, y pide que un pariente firme en la línea abajo.

______ Clasificar las palabras come hiciste en la escuela.

______ Escribir las palabras en grupos mientras las copias de las tarjetas (#1).

______ Escribir lo que aprendiste sobre palabras en esta clasificación (#2).

______ Escribir las palabras en grupos cuando alguien las dicta (#3).

______ Encontrar más palabras en la lectura que tienen el mismo sonido o patrón. Añádelas a los grupos que están atrás.

Firma de un miembro de la familia ______________________________

Word Sort Corpus

Number refers to the sort in which the word or picture appears

'd for would	49
'll for will	47, 49
n't for not	48
're for are	47
's for is	47
've for have	48
about*	54
above	54
across	54
added	59
again*	54
age	15, 44
ago	54
ahead	54
alive	54
along	54
animal	3
any	55
ape	21
apple	55
arch	45
are not	46
aren't	46, 48
around	54
asleep	54
ate	50
away*	54
baby	55
bake	21
bald	40
bar	30
bare	31, 50
barn	31
bat	4
bath	4
be	52
beach	3, 45
beaches	57
bear	50
beat	27
because*	54
bed	8
beds	57
bee	8, 52
beet	27
before*	54
began	54
begin	54
believe	54
below	54
bench	45
between	54
bike	7
bird	30, 33
birth	33
bite	20
black*	10
blew	23
blind	25
blob	11
blue	23
boar	26, 51
board	35
boat	3, 5, 16, 17
boats	57
body	55
boil	36, 37
bold	25
bolt	25
bone	5, 9, 11, 14, 16, 17, 19, 22, 37
book*	56
bore	26, 51
bored	51
born	35
both*	25
bottle	55
bought	40
box	5
boxes	57
boy*	36, 37
brain	15, 21
brake	50
branch	45
break	50
bride	7, 44
bright	24
bring	13
broke	11, 17, 22
broom	19
brought	40
bruise	18
brushes	57
bug	6
bulge	44
burn	30, 34, 58
burned	58, 59
burp	34
burst	34
bus	12
but	12
by*	24
cage	44
cake	4, 9, 10, 14, 15, 19, 21
calm	40
came*	10
cane	4, 9
can't	48
car	30, 31
care	29, 31
carrots	1
casa	28
castle	55
cat	4, 10, 14
catch	45
cauliflower	1
cause	39
cave	4, 10, 15
caza	28
celery	1
chain	9
chair	31
chairs	57
chance	14
change	44
charge	44
chase	17
cheap	27, 52
cheep	27, 52
cheer	32
chew	23
child	25
chin	7
chirp	33
chore	35
church	34, 45
churches	57
circle	2, 55
city	55
claim	21
clap	10
class	56
classes	56
claw	39
clay	21
clean	58
cleaned	58
clear	32
clerk	30, 32
climb	25
clock	5, 11, 14, 39
close	16, 51
cloth	39
clothes	51

*High Frequency Words